Your
RETIREMENT
WAKE-UP CALL

Action Steps to Retire
Healthy, Wealthy, and with **Purpose!**

Chris Ragot and Tracy Sullivan

Your Retirement Wake-Up Call: Action Steps to Retire Healthy, Wealthy, and with Purpose!
Published by Barton Creek Publishing, Ponte Vedra, Florida
Copyright ©2025 by Chris Ragot and Tracy Sullivan. All rights reserved.

ISBN: 979-8-218-74742-8

BUSINESS & ECONOMICS / Personal Finance / Retirement Planning

Cover and interior design by Rachel Valliere, copyright owned by Chris Ragot and Tracy Sullivan.
This book is not a replacement for a Certified Financial Planner (CFP)®, attorneys, insurance advisors, health coaches, or psychologists. Always seek certified professional help in creating your retirement plan.

QUANTITY PURCHASES: Schools, companies, professional groups, clubs, and other organizations may qualify for special terms when ordering quantities of this title. For information, email Hello@ YourRetirementWakeUp.com.

Printed in the United States of America.

BARTON CREEK PUBLISHING

To my wife, Susan—Although Alzheimer's disease has taken so much, your grace and strength remain with me. You gave me wings and will always be part of who I am.

To my partner, Tracy—With deep gratitude, I thank you for inspiring me to expand both my mind and my heart.

To Chris—My coconspirator in dreams and dinner plans who respects my weird, believes in my wild, and always encourages me to take action with everything I'm passionate about.

Contents

7

Five Years Out: Preplanning Your Retirement Lifestyle

8

Five Years Out: Preplanning Your Retirement Finances

9

One Year to Go: Firming Up Your Retirement Plan

10

Welcome to Your Healthy, Wealthy Retirement!

Preface:
Author Chris Ragot's
Wake-Up Call

It was the winter I reached retirement age, and I felt invincible, buoyed by good health and a sense of limitless possibility. You may be able to relate to my belief that, while our bodies age, our minds often trick us into thinking we're still twenty-five.

I'd never had a serious ski accident until a recent sunny afternoon when I agreed to take one last run down a familiar Colorado slope with my partner, Tracy.

Suddenly, I hit an icy patch, crossed my skis, went airborne, and landed in a lump on my left side. I didn't know what happened—only that my chest hurt. Tracy knew I was seriously injured when I agreed to ride down on the toboggan known to seasoned skiers like us as the "sled of shame."

After a quick assessment, ski patrol staff decided I should take an ambulance to the hospital as I might have broken some ribs, which could puncture a lung and create a medical emergency.

At the hospital, scans revealed my left clavicle was a shattered mess, and I had four broken ribs. Thankfully, my lungs were intact. Strangely, I felt relieved—it was better than the heart attack I had feared.

There's nothing much to do for broken ribs but wait for them to heal and try not to laugh or sneeze (it hurts like hell). But the clavicle was another matter.

The next day, the hospital staff prepped me for surgery. They planned to install titanium plates and screws to hold my shattered clavicle bones together. My head was spinning as they explained the procedure.

Before they gave me anesthesia, I had to sign a permission sheet acknowledging my understanding that I might die from this surgery.

Wait, I might die? That news made me run through a mental checklist:

- Do I have health insurance to cover all these expenses, along with my medical directives, so doctors know my wishes? Yes. OK, that's good.

- Are my loved ones taken care of financially? Yes, glad I've saved and have that paperwork done.

- Will I wake up? I hope I do! I haven't spoken with any of my kids since this accident, and I can't remember what I said to them the last time we talked. Did I say I love you?

Family. Health. Money. When you're staring down the possibility of your own mortality, your thoughts immediately turn to what matters most.

The fact that I'm here writing this means, yes—I woke up. But I awoke to a whirlwind of tests that confirmed what I'd been trying not to admit: I'm older than I feel, both in body and mind.

I take only one medication and have no major health issues, so I was caught off guard when the doctors raised two different concerns from test results, despite my clean bill of health just a year earlier. I knew it was time to make real changes. Better food. Less alcohol. No more half-measures—it was time to take my health seriously.

That was my wake-up call. I'd been preaching the importance of health to family and friends for years, but I wasn't exactly walking the talk.

In hindsight, the ski accident was a gift—a blunt reminder that I'm not invincible. (None of us are.) Life can change in an instant. It shattered my procrastination. I realized I'm not as young as I feel, and my recovery made that painfully clear. Let's just say I didn't bounce back like I used to.

So, I made a decision: Something had to change if I wanted to enjoy the retirement I'd worked for and be present with the people I love.

I thought I had retirement figured out. But when I finally crossed that threshold, it hit me: I was unprepared. Challenges came out of nowhere—just like that fall on the mountain.

I know I'm not alone in feeling unprepared for this whole retirement thing. If I could do it all over again, I'd approach it differently.

What would I change?

- I'd learn to understand my investments instead of trusting others to manage them.

- Five years before retirement, I'd put together a strategic retirement plan.

- Before deciding on a retirement location, I'd do more in-person research.

- I'd study up on Social Security—its benefits, deductions, and taxes.

- I'd learn about Medicare and its many health insurance options, which I didn't review until the day I needed to choose a plan.

- I'd learn how to minimize taxes in retirement.

Growing older isn't for the weak. In a culture obsessed with youth, it's easy to pretend aging won't catch up with us. But eventually, retirement shows up like a freight train, and suddenly you're hopping on, ready or not.

And if you're not ready? You're moving fast, forced to make high-stakes decisions that will shape the rest of your life. Maybe you land on your feet. Maybe you narrowly avoid a train wreck.

My ski accident happened while Tracy and I were writing this book about our retirement journey. That detour taught me even more than I expected. My hope is that by sharing what we have learned, you'll be better equipped to navigate your own road—with fewer surprises.

Welcome to Your Retirement Guidebook!

B EFORE WE DIVE into the details, we'd like to take a moment to introduce ourselves and share what motivated us to write this book. Let's start with Chris.

Hi, I'm Chris Ragot. I'm a family man, CEO, and entrepreneur who's spent most of my career building, leading, and fixing businesses. I come from humble beginnings. My parents, Pierre and Huguette Ragot, emigrated from France to the US in the 1960s when I was just seven years old.

They arrived in America as indentured servants, working as a chauffeur and maid on a Scarsdale estate near New York City. They lived in the servant's cottage, working tirelessly for five years in exchange for room and board and a chance at citizenship. They didn't make much money, but they felt lucky to have an employer willing to sponsor their future.

Eventually, my father struck out on his own as a chauffeur. My mother—now known as Yvette—launched her own business providing in-home European-style waxing.

It was a niche service back then, but word spread fast among New York City's elite.

That work ethic—that quiet grit—is what shaped me. It's what got me through college at Embry-Riddle Aeronautical University and later my MBA at Johns Hopkins University. I've founded, bought, and sold companies. I've served as CEO for others. And while I've had a good run, I'm not done yet.

You may ask why I haven't just retired, kicked back, and enjoyed the view. The truth? I'm not finished making an impact.

The idea for this book came after I turned sixty-five and found myself knee-deep in the maze of Medicare enrollment. I thought I had a solid plan for retirement, but the reality was more complicated than I had expected.

Fortunately, I'd done well financially. From that standpoint, my retirement plan was sound. But when I talked to friends, I realized many weren't so lucky. Some were struggling with money. Others with health issues. Many were lost in the transition. That's when I knew—this book needed to be written.

What struck me in conversation after conversation was this: Most people had missed at least one key element of planning and enjoying a healthy, wealthy retirement where they also enjoyed a clear sense of purpose. Some didn't save enough. Others never invested wisely. Many overlooked their health or chose to retire in places that didn't suit their lifestyle.

As I listened to their stories—stories of struggle, disappointment, and unrealized expectations—I started asking deeper questions.

This is when Tracy and I became amateur social scientists. We wanted to understand, in a country as wealthy as ours, why so many people are struggling with retirement. What is getting in the way of living by their values, protecting their health, building strong relationships, and enjoying the freedom they'd worked for?

Tracy's turn to introduce herself!

Hi, I'm Tracy Sullivan. Raised as a latchkey kid in Chicago, I worked my way through college, bootstrapped a successful photography business, and lived solo for over a decade. I believe that kind of independence builds perseverance and independent thinking. It also enables me to bring a sharp and grounded perspective to our research. Plus, I bring the insight and intuition of a woman's point of view to the discussion about creating the life you want to live in retirement. A life with a clear sense of purpose. A life that reflects your values.

Together, we make a great team. As we sought to understand people's retirement challenges, including why they put off planning for so long (if they plan at all!), we were always asking questions, whether we were out to dinner with friends, chatting with strangers on the ski slopes, or visiting family.

With younger people, we'd dig in with questions that would prompt them to think about retirement: Are you looking forward to retirement? Do you think you're saving enough? Do you believe Social Security will still be there when it's time to retire?

For older people, our questions were along these lines: How is retirement treating you? Do you have enough money to support the lifestyle you want? How is your health? Are you happy living where you live? Did you have to downsize? What is your purpose in retirement? Do you miss working?

Many of the answers were troubling. We heard a variety of distressing comments, such as:

- "I'll start saving for retirement later, once my career takes off."

- "I've had to go back to work at seventy-five."

- "Living off Social Security is harder than I thought it would be."

- "I chose the wrong place to retire."

We wondered if we were getting a skewed view of the so-called golden years. Were the people in our orbit unusual?

We dug into retirement research, and it reinforced what we'd heard. The statistics about Americans' lack of retirement preparation are flat-out shocking:

- One in five people over age fifty have no retirement savings (AARP).

- More than half of Americans are one missed paycheck away from homelessness (the US Interagency Council on Homelessness).

- Financial forecasts predict that 45 percent of us will outlive our savings (MarketWatch).

- The median savings for fifty-five-year-olds is only $10,000 (Prudential).

- Only 55 percent of Gen Xers participate in company retirement plans (National Institute on Retirement Security).

- Close to one-third of Americans are worried their poor health could endanger their retirement plans (CNBC).

- Approximately one-third of adults worldwide are not meeting the recommended levels of physical activity, putting billions of people worldwide at risk of serious illness (World Health Organization).

- Nearly one-third (28 percent) of retirees report they're depressed (National Library of Medicine).

To sum this up, many Americans are wildly unprepared for retirement. Few are laying the groundwork for a vibrant retirement—one where they have a clear sense of purpose, have enough money, and are healthy enough to enjoy it.

Another big problem? Nobody walks you through the decisions you need to make when you retire, and in a couple of cases, those decisions need to happen at precise points in time.

We thought we could find a wholistic guide that would walk us through it all. So, we went looking for that book.

A Whole-Person Retirement Answer Book

As you've probably guessed, we couldn't find the book we wanted. We wanted a book that would cover:

- How to avoid pitfalls that could derail your retirement

- How to save and invest for retirement

- Tips to maintain good physical and mental health as you age
- The key elements you need to feel satisfied in your golden years
- The steps to create a smooth retirement transition

Instead, we found a mountain of books about saving and investing. We tripped over tons of exercise and diet books for all ages. We unearthed studies aplenty about which factors create good mental health in retirement. *However, no single book brought all the information together.*

This book is the wholistic retirement planning guide we've all been searching for. This book will help you plan for and live a retirement life that's healthy, wealthy, and brimming with a clear sense of purpose. In addition, this book is our wake-up call for you—we urge you to start your retirement planning and saving *now*, no matter how young or old you are.

In these pages, you'll find real-life stories from both of us and the people we've interviewed. While we've changed everyone's names and altered some details to protect their privacy, the essence of each story is 100 percent true. This book is a collection of hard-won wisdom we wish we'd known sooner.

Financial planners rarely discuss nutrition, and fitness experts don't ask about your investment strategy. But, in reality, you need all the pieces for a retirement that works. There's no point in saving $1 million if by age sixty-five you're alone, sick, and unhappy.

A caveat: We're not accountants or lawyers and don't know your particular situation. Please seek professional advice as you make important financial, health, and life decisions.

Think of this book as a layperson's guide to the real world of retirement—your planning guide to figure out your life's direction and your finances as early as you can, so your retirement rocks. We are nearing or just past retirement age as we write this, and we are "opening the kimono" to share what we've learned along the way.

Life's a Game

In many ways, life resembles a game of Chutes and Ladders. (If you are from Australia, Canada, the UK, or India, you may know this game as Snakes and Ladders.) This idea became a guiding principle for this book.

In life, we can encounter helpful ladders that create shortcuts past some of the hard slogging of life. Or we can encounter chutes, those mistakes or unforeseen circumstances that send us sliding back to Start again.

Each chapter in this book gives you tools to help you find more helpful ladders up and avoid all the chutes you can, including backup plans to help you sidestep any unforeseen chutes. Things like taking a bad fall on a snowy mountainside.

This Book Is for You If . . .

Since you're reading this book, you probably have one or more of these topics on your mind. You may be:

- Worried you won't have enough money put away to retire comfortably—or at all

- Concerned you don't understand finances and investing
- Thinking Social Security or Medicare won't be there when you retire
- Planning on Social Security as your sole retirement income
- Confused about when to sign up for Medicare or begin taking Social Security
- Concerned about your purpose after retirement
- Wondering if you'll need to downsize
- Unsure where you should retire
- Uncomfortable discussing money matters with family
- Unclear on how early to start planning for retirement
- Unsure how to stay healthy in old age
- Experiencing anxiety about retirement
- Thinking it's too early (or too late) to save for retirement
- Inexperienced with long-range planning

If any of these concerns resonate with you, this book should help you gain clarity. It offers a step-by-step planning guide to create the best retirement you possibly can, starting from the stage of life you are in right now—without waiting until you're on retirement's doorstep.

Four Ways to Use This Book

Rather than organize this book by age groups, the chapters cover seven major life stages on the road to retirement. People go through phases at different speeds and retire at different ages, so this approach made sense to us.

Whatever your current life stage, you can:

1. **Read the book from the beginning**—If you're a younger person, this is our recommended approach. If you're past the earlier stages of life, you'll still gather a substantial number of tips to prepare for your retirement and to share with younger friends or your adult children.

2. **Jump straight to the chapter for your current stage**—Start at "your" chapter and read on from there. Although, if you're near or at retirement, don't skip the Five Years Out chapters, which offer a ton of useful planning tips even if you're past that five-year point.

3. **Take the skimmer's approach**—Scan through to check out the stories and watch for our top takeaways at the end of each chapter. But keep in mind, reading this entire planning guide will give you more details that tell you exactly how and when to take important actions.

4. **Take action with the free accompanying workbook**—We've gathered many of the action items in this book as well as key questions to ask to plan your retirement into a comprehensive workbook, which you'll find on our informative website, www.YourRetirementWakeUp.com.

The first important stage to build a healthy, wealthy retirement that's brimming with a clear sense of purpose begins when you complete your schooling and start working. So, we'll start there.

2

Just Starting Out—
Get a Firm Footing
for the Path Ahead

Here you are, perhaps in your twenties or thirties, reading a retirement planning guide. We're proud of you! At this stage of your life, it's incredibly important to establish a solid foundation for the rest of your life and, eventually, for a happy and secure retirement. Yes, retirement seems like a million years away, but trust us, it sneaks up on you fast!

To help you establish a firm footing, this chapter is packed with a ton of practical information you can immediately put to use, including career advice, tips to stay healthy, and a crash course on saving and investing money. Hint: Start saving now! It makes all the difference. (If you're older and reading this chapter, welcome! You'll find useful information for any age group.)

Let's start by addressing the significant difference between having a job or career—and why a career will help you achieve the good life for decades to come.

A Critical First Step: Career Versus Job

In the working world, everyone starts somewhere. You could find yourself working at a fast-food restaurant, as a receptionist, or in retail. You need money, so you apply everywhere and take whatever comes your way—for the time being. There's no shame in honest work. The trick is to move up from those first jobs and build a career that brings you joy, one you can advance in over the years.

What's the difference between a job and a career? A job pays this month's bills. A career, according to Merriam-Webster's dictionary, is "a profession for which one trains, and which is undertaken as a permanent calling."

Building your career may require more effort up front, but it's likely to pay off in the long run. If your first role in your chosen field doesn't offer a higher salary than your initial jobs, don't get discouraged. Climbing the career ladder typically leads to greater earnings over time, while a job often doesn't offer much in terms of increased pay or responsibilities.

You'll need the higher income a career offers to save for emergencies—and for retirement. No matter what you're doing now to pay the bills, ask yourself: Where is this headed? If the answer is nowhere, it's time to change direction.

According to a 2021 survey conducted by the Georgetown University Center on Education and the Workforce, in today's tech-driven economy, career opportunities often require post-high school education or specialized training. By 2031, 72 percent of jobs will require more than just a high school diploma.

Maybe you'll be the exception and bootstrap your way into your chosen career—more power to you. Perhaps you'll start out parking cars and work your way up, eventually owning your own car service. But keep in mind, it's becoming increasingly difficult to earn a good income without some form of advanced education.

If you're in a job and uncertain whether it leads to a career you want, it's time to get clear. Career-track jobs typically offer the stability and resources that will help you earn money for those rainy days and for retirement while helping you maintain your health over the long term.

Healthy Body, Healthy Bank Account

When it comes to your health, you can choose one of two basic paths: Either you have health insurance, or you don't.

To understand the impact of going through life without health insurance, let's follow a young man we'll call Joe. He just landed an entry-level accounting job after earning his bachelor's degree. Joe is a fun-loving guy who enjoys late nights out, eating and drinking with friends without a second thought.

You may think he's too young to face health issues, but you'd be wrong. Poor lifestyle choices like Joe's are contributing to an increase in serious diseases among younger people, including heart disease and diabetes.

One day, Joe notices he feels dizzy whenever he skips a meal, and he is constantly thirsty. He decides to see his primary care doctor. After running a few tests, the doctor diagnoses Joe with diabetes, caused by his poor diet and excessive drinking. The doctor prescribes medication and gives him a plan for healthier eating and exercise, offering Joe a chance to reverse the course of the disease. Fortunately, Joe's out-of-pocket costs are minimal as his health insurance covers most of the expenses.

Now, let's imagine a different scenario. Joe didn't go to college and works as a seasonal groundskeeper at the local golf course. When he starts experiencing the same symptoms, he has no health insurance, just like about 8 percent of American families. Without insurance, Joe faces much higher out-of-pocket costs and potentially delayed care.

This means he doesn't see a doctor regularly. In fact, he doesn't have a primary care physician who could observe that his health is going downhill. And it's unlikely he'll seek out a doctor to investigate his symptoms since he'll have to pay cash for that expensive doctor's visit. Without knowledge of his developing diabetes, he'll probably continue his current habits, possibly until he turns up in an ER in a diabetic coma.

If Joe manages to pull through that diabetic crisis, he'll leave the hospital with a whopping bill no one will help him pay. Now, Joe has medical debt that he'll struggle to pay off with his low income. He has tumbled down a major financial chute.

According to the Kauffman Family Foundation, you're more than twice as likely to postpone help or not see a doctor at all when you're uninsured. That's a big gamble to take with your health. If your job doesn't come with health insurance, prioritize paying for it yourself. Yes, it's a major expense, but it's a must-have item in your budget. Access to healthcare is a key reason we advocate pursuing a career and not just clocking in to a job.

Inside Your Company's Healthcare Plan

According to a US Census Bureau report, just over half of Americans have company-sponsored healthcare plans, but few use all the available benefits. Be the exception and read the fine print because many corporations are beefing up their preventive health and wellness programs. Our research reveals that more corporations are embracing wellness programs to improve the overall health of their workforce and, ultimately, save on healthcare costs.

Corporate perks may include access to a gym or online exercise classes, support groups, lunchtime walking groups, sports contests, weight-loss challenges, and more. Participate in their wellness activities to develop better health habits. Illness prevention may seem burdensome, but building healthy habits pays massive dividends.

We can't leave this little wellness chat without a word on one other important health habit. Put down the Cheetos a sec, and let's talk about what you're eating.

How to Build Healthy Eating Habits

Dietary habits from childhood can greatly impact adult eating choices. For example, those who grew up with takeout options, such as pizza and fried chicken, may lean toward convenient foods, such as ramen and donuts, in college. Conversely, individuals who ate healthily at home may find themselves switching to fast food, such as burgers and fries, once they start working. Recognizing these patterns is important to foster healthier eating habits.

Those of us who've buried friends who died young know how essential good health is for a happy life and retirement. A friend's classmate died from complications of obesity—at age thirty-seven.

Here are our top three tips on how to build healthier eating habits:

1. **Pick one thing to change at a time**—Don't overload yourself by trying to change fifteen things at once. Maybe you decide to stop buying soft drinks. A week later, change one more thing; perhaps you cut out after-dinner snacking. Baby steps add up to big changes when it comes to eating habits.

2. **Don't wait until you have health problems to start making changes**—The longer you persist on a junk-food diet, the harder it'll be to switch. Find healthy foods you love now, and make them your usual choices.

3. **Stay informed**—Subscribe to some of the top online consumer health newsletters, such as Healthline and WebMD. New studies come out all the time, which can inspire you to switch up your health habits.

As a society, we continue to learn more about how to eat healthily. What's the latest info? Here are a few tidbits:

- What you eat affects your gut microbiome, which in turn affects nearly every aspect of your health and, according to a 2020 article in the *Journal of Neuroinflammation*, your mental health, too!

- Eating more fiber-filled veggies, fruits, and grains builds a healthy gut biome. Eating a lot of chemical-ridden, ultra-processed foods your grandma wouldn't recognize does not.

- Eating tons of animal protein makes you a candidate for heart disease.

- The hormones you ingest in most beef and dairy products today are a proven cause of tumors, according to a 2014 National Library of Medicine article.

Besides a lifetime of overeating and poor nutrition, a couple of other common habits could kill you. If you're puffing on a cigarette with a cocktail in your hand, read on.

Breaking the Bad Habits

Alcohol use can destroy your health as well as your relationships and your career. The latest thinking is that the only safe amount of alcohol to consume is *none*. World Health Organization researchers presented their findings in an article with this definitive title: "No Level of Alcohol Consumption is Safe for Our Health."

We appreciate good wine and the occasional cocktail, recognizing that spending time with friends over a drink or two is a social activity. However, we also acknowledge that completely avoiding alcohol may not be realistic for everyone. As we grow older, we've found ourselves cutting back on drinking as it can take a toll on our bodies.

The good news is that we're seeing a growing movement toward alcohol-free enjoyment. You can embrace the Dry January or Sober Curious movements and savor delicious craft mocktails, which contain no alcohol. It is entirely possible to be social and have a fantastic time without alcohol.

Let's turn our attention to another unhealthy habit. Unlike the recent news on the effects of alcohol use, the fact that smoking kills has been widely known since the

1960s. Sadly, nearly half a million people have died from their habit since then, many of whom died from lung cancer. If you're in your twenties or thirties, take note—that's the age when most smokers get hooked, according to the Centers for Disease Control and Prevention (CDC).

Tracy has personal experience with the terrible realities of lung cancer due to her mother's history of smoking. Her mother smoked for thirty years. For many of those years, she woke up coughing and feeling unwell. Unfortunately, her elderly doctor, whom she revered, misdiagnosed her worsening symptoms as bronchitis.

At the urging of her family, she sought a second opinion, but it was too late. She was diagnosed with an aggressive form of small-cell lung cancer that had metastasized to her brain in just over two years. She passed away at the young age of sixty-four. We lost a beautiful soul who could have made changes in her life. And you can as well. Take a moment to think about it.

This may sound like a public service announcement, but if you smoke, it's time to quit. Additionally, if you have a persistent health condition that isn't improving, please don't ignore it. Get it checked out, and you'll be relieved if it turns out to be nothing or grateful if an issue is caught early.

Maintaining healthy exercise habits is vital as well. Beyond disease prevention, one of the benefits of exercise is that it helps to calm your mind. Developing awareness of your thoughts and feelings is an important skill that can assist you in every aspect of your life, contributing to a happier life and leading to a happier retirement. Being aware of your thoughts and feelings leads us to our next topic, which is often overlooked in health discussions.

What's Your EQ?

Some people like to brag about their IQ. But researchers have identified another kind of smarts that is possibly more important. It's emotional intelligence or emotional quotient (EQ). Psychologist Daniel Goleman popularized this concept in the 1990s in his book, *Emotional Intelligence: Why It Can Matter More Than IQ.*

Goleman asserts that people with high EQ are better able to build and maintain relationships, both at work and at home.

What is EQ? Here are four aspects to master:

1. **Self-awareness**—Understand your strengths and weaknesses, recognizing your emotions and how they impact others.

2. **Self-management**—Manage your emotions, so you can stay calm and upbeat in stressful situations.

3. **Social awareness**—This is the ability to recognize and empathize with others' feelings.

4. **Relationship management**—Apply your emotional awareness to improve your relationships, which enables you to resolve conflicts and more effectively mentor others.

If you're wondering why we're talking about EQ in a retirement planning book, well, if you're aware of your feelings, it's a lot easier to plan a retirement you'll enjoy! It's hard to make future plans if you don't know whether your current lifestyle makes you happy or sad. And, of course, exhibiting emotional intelligence gives you a clear advantage when you're pursuing a career versus working a job.

Has a troubled childhood, relationship issues, or other life trauma disconnected you from your feelings? We encourage you to work on reconnecting through therapy, group support, apps, or whatever you need. That emotional self-knowledge is essential to master self-control and enhance your EQ.

Once you know yourself, look outward. You'll be better at reading the room and leading a team at work when you can tune into others' emotions. EQ skills will also help you improve your personal and work relationships, step up as a leader, resolve conflicts, and build intimacy.

Build Your Self-Awareness

Few of us are born with high EQ. It takes time, practice, and life experience to tune in to our emotions and those of others. But it's worth it to gain better self-awareness and stronger relationships in your personal and professional life.

Tracy says much of her EQ developed in the decade she lived alone after ending a fourteen-year relationship. Friends would often tell her, "You're so strong!" when they saw her dealing with difficult life situations. Over time, she realized a lot of that perceived strength was actually a facade—she was suppressing negative past experiences rather than confronting them.

Eventually, she realized her fears from those past experiences made her question whether history would repeat itself. As a result, she carried anxiety from previous relationships into new ones. If you're not careful, this type of baggage can poison a promising new romance.

To move forward, she found an online resource with a workbook and videos focused on processing past trauma.

She recalls that each morning of the five-day program, she sat at her kitchen table, reflecting, crying, and writing. This painful work helped her develop self-awareness and better emotional intelligence, allowing her to explore her fears more deeply. Confronting her past, she says, helped her let go of old hurts and solidify her core values.

She adds that when she stopped compartmentalizing her emotions and identified her true values she was able to heal. This new awareness helped her build stronger, deeper connections with those around her, free from fear.

Never stop learning about yourself—it's the only way to grow. It's OK to acknowledge that you need help recovering from past hurts. For many of us, this is the hardest step in learning about ourselves. Take the leap. It's worth it.

What's your EQ? You can find several self-assessments online that can give you a baseline. Then, work on improvement. Ask yourself if you:

- Are aware of how you're feeling

- Are a good listener

- Keep emotional reactions in check

- Show empathy toward others

As you get in touch with your feelings and build your EQ, this will help clarify an important aspect of any happy life: understanding what you value most.

Clarify Your Values Today for a Better Tomorrow

Here's an important question to ask yourself: Is how I spend my time aligned with what really matters to me?

Let us gently encourage you to reflect on this question. Addressing this question now—and taking steps to align how you spend your time with what matters to you—will improve your odds of building a fulfilling life and a retirement you enjoy.

When we talk about what really matters to you, we're talking about values. What are values? They're deeply ingrained principles that guide all your actions. Or they *should* guide your actions.

Clarifying your most important, core values will help you plan for the future. Your core values are the scaffold on which to build your life. But if you don't live by those beliefs, it's easy to end up somewhere unintended—and less pleasant.

It's time to define your core values. Begin by brainstorming a list of everything you care about. Your list may include multiple entries, such as:

- Marriage
- Family
- Faith
- Spirituality
- Children
- Friendship
- Avoiding drama
- Spending time in nature
- Physical activity
- Taking care of your body
- Frugality
- Hard work
- Job security
- Travel
- Creativity
- Fame
- Financial wealth
- Professional accomplishment
- A large circle of friends
- Avoiding stress
- Intellectual stimulation

- Kindness
- Compassion
- Forgiveness
- Listening to others
- Honesty
- Resilience
- Authenticity
- Being a good listener

Once you brainstorm ideas, narrow them down to a top ten list. These are your core values.

If you're stuck, ask yourself these questions: What would I be deeply unhappy without? What would I consider a horrible loss if it never happens over the course of my life?

Get clarity on your values now. If you wait to define your values until later in life, changing course can be hard.

BIG TIP: Print out your list of core values and post it in a prominent place at home for frequent review.

Once you're aware of your values, think about the current direction of your life. Are your actions aligned with your values? If not, something needs to change.

With clarity on your core values, you can set goals for living by them. A lot of people get values and goals confused, so let's clarify the difference.

What You Want Versus How You Get It

Here's how values are different from goals:

- Values are your guide for how best to live your life.

- Goals are future destinations you plan to reach.

Basing your life around values is far more satisfying than relying on goals as Dr. Russ Harris explains in his book and course, *The Happiness Trap: How to Stop Struggling and Start Living*.

Well-defined values help you become your best self. Values help you stay true to yourself when things go sideways in life, which they will.

Goals are a search for an end result. You hope to be happy when you achieve your goal.

Here's the problem: Achieving a goal gives you fleeting joy. You need to keep setting new goals to get that achievement high again.

When you live your values, you can enjoy every moment of your journey instead of postponing happiness—sometimes for years—while you work to meet a hoped-for goal. Values also shape the future you create.

The North Star to Define Your Future

Values are your internal navigation system for what you want to do with your life. Your values are like the tow-rope on a ski hill. You latch on and that rope guides you straight to the top of the run. You don't end up lost in the wilderness.

Now that you've clarified your values, hang onto your list, so you can revisit it every five years or so because your values will change. For instance, if you're just out of college and frugality is a big value for you, you may be living at home with your parents to save money. Or maybe family is a core value, and it's your culture's custom to live at home until you get married.

But will you still want to live with your parents when you're thirty? How about forty? Probably not. By then, values such as independence or building your own family may be more important. You'll sacrifice the low cost of staying home to fulfill those new values and their related goals.

Sometimes, creating the life you want requires sacrifice, especially when you want to attain a challenging goal. One of our friends wanted to be a pilot but could barely afford flight school. So, he gave up his apartment and slept in his car while he got that training. He's been a pilot for Southwest Airlines for over a decade now, enjoying his dream career and all the perks that come with it.

Now that you understand how values and goals work in your life, let's bring them together and plan the lifestyle you want.

Get on an Exciting and Profitable Path

If your life has fallen into a numbing routine of work, sleep, eat, repeat—stop a minute. It's time to make a five-year plan. Without a plan, you may wake up five years from now in exactly the same spot. Why five years? It's a fairly short timeline that enables you to think about where you'd like to be in just a few years.

Let's make sure your values and the related goals you set will help you make progress toward the life you want. Self-awareness isn't a big value in our culture these days, so give yourself an edge by taking time to check in with yourself and then taking time to plan your future.

Creating this five-year plan is a basic adulting step. It's figuring out who you are, what you want, and the steps to get there.

Imagine it's a few years from now, and you're living your ideal life. Where are you, who are you with, and how do you spend your work and leisure time? Your five-year plan should show you whether your current routine will lead where you want to go—or if you've gotten sidetracked or stuck.

Here are some things to think about as you imagine your life a half-decade from now:

- Where do I want to live?
- Who do I want to be with?
- Am I looking to find a partner? Get married?
- What sort of work do I want to do?
- What would I like to do in my leisure time?
- How much money do I want to have saved?
- How much do I need to save monthly to achieve that goal?
- What are the specific goals that could serve as milestones to achieve my five-year plan?

As you can see, your five-year plan covers much more than money goals. It should paint a full picture of the future life you want.

Without a plan, it's easy to wander off course when life happens. This happened to a bright, young bartender who waits on us at our favorite upscale restaurant in our hometown. We'll call her Lucy. Listen in on our conversation to see how Lucy's lack of a five-year plan left her stuck.

———————— ☕ ————————

Tracy: Hi Lucy. We'll have our usual glass of wine and beer.

Lucy: Here you go.

Chris: [Sips a beer] Lucy, I'm curious, if you don't mind my asking, do you make a good living bartending here?

Lucy: Sure do! I made about $100,000 last year.

Tracy: Are you going to college, too?

Lucy: I started out that way, but right now I'm just bartending.

Chris: Oh? What were you studying?

Lucy: I got a BA in mathematics. I really want to be a civil engineer, you know, build bridges. But I'd need a master's degree. Right now, the money here is too good to turn down.

Tracy: Hey, I get it. I have a friend in Chicago who tended bar in college, then went back to school and became a certified mixologist. Now he makes well over $100,000 a year. Do you see yourself moving up to be a food and beverage manager or maybe a sommelier?

Lucy: I'd probably be happier in engineering. It would be more challenging. I won't want to wait on difficult, tipsy people until two in the morning when I'm in my forties. But it'd be hard to switch careers now because my first engineering job would pay less than what I'm making now.

Chris: Sure, but what kind of benefits package do you get here? Does this bar have a 401(k) plan with matching contributions from your employer? Paid vacation or sick time or personal days? Do you have opportunities for advancement? Civil engineers tend to work for governments, and the benefits are usually terrific.

Lucy: [Laughs] I never compared the two careers that way. I've been feeling like I'm stuck in a loop.

Chris: Could you cut expenses for a while and save for your master's degree? You could always supplement your income while in college by bartending once or twice a week.

Lucy: [Thinks a beat] I guess I could. My place is big. I could get a roommate for a while and cut back on travel. Maybe I should take a look at the master's program deadlines at my university.

Right now, high income is important to Lucy, but she can see that professional fulfillment will become more important over time. It's time for Lucy to make a change. She can start by clarifying her values, identifying specific goals, and writing down her five-year plan. Realistically, in five years she could have her master's degree; could be working a fulfilling, challenging job as a civil engineer; and could be earning more than her current take-home pay—with benefits! Or she could still be tending bar.

BIG TIP: Having a job is good. Having a career is better!

The Road to the Life You Want

Now that you've worked on your five-year plan, take a look at your hoped-for life a few years out. How does your future vision square with how you spend your time now?

If you continue in your current job, where will you be in five years? Does your current job offer opportunities for growth, advancement, and a rewarding career? Maybe you've gotten a taste of corporate life and see that it's not for you. If so, a technical or trade school program could steer you in a new direction.

Or maybe your current career is a financial dead-end. When Chris started out as a pilot, he realized the earning potential was limited. Since he wanted a better lifestyle, he switched his focus to business.

To make a change, you have to build a bridge from the road you've been on to a new one. Sometimes, it's hard because you may not have parents, friends, or mentors to guide and support this transition.

Tracy shares that she comes from a background where no one talked about pursuing a career. No one ever explained the difference between a job and a career, much less the importance of college. She remembers buying patterns and cheap fabric to make her own clothes for fun and even wearing some of her creations to school. Yet no one thought to buy her a sewing machine or encourage her to attend design school.

Her father's advice was simple but unhelpful: "You're cute—just get married and have children."

She floundered, in part due to an early diagnosis of dyslexia and the struggle to find her own way of handling it. Eventually, she discovered a college photography course, but it didn't quite fit her personality and style. However, a trade school that focused on photography did, and for the first time, things began to make sense. Still, without guidance, she made plenty of unnecessary missteps.

Chris recalls that his parents were often critical of his ambitions. They questioned why he was wasting time and money on college, which he was paying for himself. His mother wanted him to become a plumber. When he told his parents he was going to Embry-Riddle Aeronautical University to get his pilot's license and college degree, his father's reaction wasn't encouragement. Instead, he said, "You want to be a pilot? You wouldn't be good at that—you're not smart enough. You'll hurt somebody."

If these scenarios sound familiar, tap into other resources for career mentors. Take an extension course or join a support group. Talk with adults in your neighborhood or place of worship. Most people are happy to give career advice to younger people looking for input and direction.

Thinking of starting a business? Take a class on business start-ups, and seek out your local district office of Small Business Development Centers, a program supported by the US Small Business Administration (www.sba.gov). You'll find mentors there for entrepreneurship.

Continuing down a dead-end road is a complete waste of time. But sometimes, it's hard to understand what you need to do instead. Chris's conversation with a friend's son provided a classic example. Anthony wanted to talk with him about careers because he's interested in joining a high-powered financial firm when he graduates. Here, Chris relates a portion of his discussion with Anthony.

———— ☕ ————

"That's a great goal," I said. "Where are you going to school now?"

Anthony proudly named the local state university—not a terrible choice for many college majors, but it's not a place that gets you hired at a leading, global financial firm. All those movers and shakers have degrees from top business schools, such as Harvard and Wharton.

"Where are you working this summer?" I asked him.

"I got a job as a caddy," he replied. "It's pretty easy, and I'm even getting a tan!"

At this, I could only sigh. This young man is wasting his time, I thought. Starting many months ago, Anthony should have worked aggressively to arrange a summer internship in finance at a large and respected firm. Neither his current college nor his summer work choice supports his four-year goal of landing a high-paying job in a high-powered financial firm immediately after graduation. He's living in a dream world.

There's still time for Anthony to get on a proven path into a major financial firm, but his window of opportunity is closing. He would need to transfer to a new school and land relevant internships while he's still an undergraduate. Like so many people, he doesn't understand how important it is to build a bridge from the road he's on to a new road that leads to the future he envisions. After graduation, if he cannot break into his desired career, it'll be a lot harder to start on a new career ladder. He may have more responsibilities by then, making it harder to go back to school to attain the new career's educational requirements.

BIG TIP: Continuing down a dead-end road is a waste of time. You need to create your five-year plan and get on the road that will take you where you want to go. Remember, you only have so long to earn and put aside the money you'll live on in retirement. That day may seem like a million years away, but the easiest way to retire rich (and early!) is to start socking away money now. It's time to learn some financial basics to help you get started.

Money Facts: A Crash Course

Because our nation fails spectacularly at teaching financial literacy in high school, most of us leave high school or even college with little money savvy. In case you feel confused or clueless or just need a refresher course, here's a money management primer to help you build good financial habits.

To start, here are a few basic concepts you need to understand:

- **Bank accounts**—If you're unbanked, get a checking account and a high-yield savings account for your emergency money.

- **Budgeting**—Track your expenses and income to make sure you're not living beyond your means. If you are, either cut back on your expenses or figure out how to earn more.

- **Credit cards**—Stick to one card that offers the best perks and strive to pay off your balance each month, so you don't pay interest charges.

- **Credit ratings**—Make on-time payments, so you maintain good credit, which will help you borrow at lower interest rates. Wondering what your credit rating is now? You can get a free annual copy of your credit reports from all three major credit bureaus at www.AnnualCreditReport.com.

- **Debt**—Avoid it if you can, especially high-interest debt, such as payday loans and credit card debt. If you have debt, look to consolidate it, negotiate better terms, and pay it off as fast as you can.

- **Emergency fund**—Don't live one paycheck from homelessness. Build up a savings account with enough to cover three to six months of expenses.

Once you have a handle on those fundamentals, a few more financial concepts are important for you to know. For instance, let's take a look at what you're buying and whether it's hurting your savings efforts or helping.

Your Nest Egg: Get It Going, Get It Growing

As consumers, we can choose to make two types of purchases—good choices that grow in value over time and poor choices that lose value. For example, when you invest in stocks, a high-yield savings account, or buy real estate, you're hoping these assets will be worth more as time goes on. In addition, real estate is an appreciating asset that helps you build wealth for retirement. Owning property lets you build equity, and you could rent it out for extra income. It may grow in value over time, so you can sell it for a nice profit. These are all examples of wise purchases, investments, and appreciating assets.

On the other hand, if you buy a flashy new car, it's worth less the minute you drive it off the lot. For every year you own it, its value declines further. It's a depreciating asset.

Assets that appreciate will help you start saving for and building your retirement nest egg. They provide a shortcut to wealth, a ladder that will help you save for a secure retirement.

Assets that depreciate rob you of cash, which you could have invested for the future. So, spend with care and don't make purchases based on emotion—or the color of that flashy new car!

Here's a quick example: Tracy once owned a home filled with unhappy memories from a past relationship. After her relationship ended, she decided to sell the property and move away. Now, she wishes she had renovated the second-floor garage apartment to earn rental income. The house would have appreciated in value, and she could have benefited from years of rental payments.

Try not to act on emotion when it comes to money. Before you make a big purchase, ask yourself if this is an investment that will grow in value over time or if it's money down the drain.

We know it's hard when you've just started working, but you want to sock away all the money you can while you're young. Let's talk about all the reasons why.

The Magic of Starting Now

When you're in your first job, it feels like you have decades to acquire good financial habits and save for retirement. But it's an illusion. In fact, starting to save while you're young is the best opportunity to build a fat savings account for your secure retirement—a chance you'll never have again.

How much should you be saving? A 2025 T. Rowe Price article estimates you should have eleven times your ending salary saved up for a comfortable retirement. Yes, you don't know what you'll ultimately earn. But it should be far more than you make at the outset of your career. The easiest way to meet that eleven-times goal? Save 15 percent of your salary per year, starting now. If you can't save that much, put away what you can. Saving now makes achieving your retirement savings goals easier, thanks to the magic of compounding interest.

Interest on Interest: Understand Compounding

Here's how your savings grow: Banks pay you monthly interest on all the money you have in your savings account. The next month, it pays interest on your principal *and* on the interest you earned last month.

Repeat this magic of compounding interest over many months and years, and you'll accelerate your growth rate because you're being paid interest on interest. The earlier you start saving, the more years of compound interest you'll have to grow your money before you retire.

In the previous pages, we mentioned the importance of having an emergency fund. The goal is to build up a savings account with enough to cover three to six months of expenses since, as you know, life happens. Have you built that emergency fund yet? If so, congrats! It'll grow over time.

Now you can move on to creating a retirement account. It's time to move beyond simply saving to investing your money.

How to Grow Money Faster

To build your emergency savings, you may have used a money market or high-interest savings account. As we write this, a high-yield savings account pays about 5 percent interest.

When you're saving for retirement, you can think long term and start investing your money. You can take on a bit more risk in hopes of beating that 5 percent. Stock market investing is a common way to do that.

To choose investments, you'll need to clarify your money values. Are you risk averse or willing to take on some risk for higher returns? Study the options and find your comfort zone.

Don't be fooled—it's not too early to invest for retirement. To illustrate, let's return to the story of Joe and his two possible careers as a low-paid groundskeeper or a more highly paid, college-educated accountant.

First, let's look at accountant Joe's options. We'll assume he invests in a fairly conservative, mixed-stock portfolio—the kind that tracks the Standard and Poor's 500 stock market index and historically sees an average 8 percent annual growth. The catch? Stock markets move up and down, so your return in any given year may be much lower or higher.

With his $80,000 annual income, Joe can make an initial deposit of $5,000 and then invest $5,000 per year—about $420 a month—over forty-five years. Here's how much money Joe will have when he retires at sixty-five if he starts this retirement-savings plan at twenty, thirty, or fifty years old and gets the average annual return of approximately 8 percent:

Accountant Joe starts saving at twenty years old: $2,250,000

Accountant Joe starts saving at thirty years old: $1,004,000

Accountant Joe starts saving at fifty years old: $162,500

Were you shocked at how much less accountant Joe will have saved for retirement if he waits until he's fifty years old? It's simple math. If you only have fifteen years for your money to grow, you will see far less return than if you have forty-five years.

On the other hand, the situation for groundskeeper Joe is bleak, even if he starts saving for retirement at age twenty. He has much less money to invest due to his lower income of $42,000 a year. He can only afford to save $1,000 initially, plus $1,000 a year.

Here's how much he will save if he retires at sixty-five, based on the same approximately 8 percent average stock market growth:

Groundskeeper Joe starts saving at twenty years old: $450,000

Groundskeeper Joe starts saving at thirty years old: $201,000

Groundskeeper Joe starts saving at fifty years old: $32,500

As you can see, the sooner you start investing your retirement funds, the more money you'll have when you retire. If groundskeeper Joe doesn't start saving for retirement until he's fifty, he will only have $32,500 saved for retirement. This simply would not provide a comfortable and secure retirement for him. In fact, he would probably need to work well beyond the age of sixty-five to cover basic living expenses.

Remember, if you have a company 401(k) plan with an employer matching contribution, take the match. This is free money deposited into your retirement account that increases your annual savings. Don't understand the investing choices in your 401(k)? Ask for a meeting with the company's financial advisor.

Learn investing basics—seek to understand mutual funds, exchange-traded funds (ETFs), and how portfolio diversification works as you age. Be an informed investor.

Will Social Security Be There for You?

While we find it hard to believe our politicians will let Social Security go bankrupt or that they'll succeed in privatizing it, the majority of people in the Gen Z and Millennial generations worry that this national program won't exist by the time they're old enough to benefit.

If you're worried, too, what can you do? Understand that paying for retirement may be entirely up to you. Which means you should save and invest even more than your parents did to secure your retirement.

Top Ten Takeaways for Younger Workers

What are the most important things to know and actions to take during this stage of life? Here's our top ten list:

1. **You don't want a job**—You want a career.

2. **Have health insurance**—Use it preventively to monitor your health.

3. **Eat healthily and exercise**—It'll help protect you from disease and medical debt.

4. **Create healthy habits**—Think about all the facets of good health, including eating, drinking, your social network, mental health, and not smoking.

5. **Develop your emotional quotient (EQ)**—It'll increase your success at work and in your relationships.

6. **Define your core values**—Next, create goals that will help you live those values.

7. **Make a five-year plan**—This will help you define where you want to go and identify any bridges you need to build to get there.

8. **Create a budget**—Once you know your income and spending, commit to living beneath your means, so you can build an emergency fund.

9. **Master financial basics**—Understand how bank accounts, compound interest, appreciation, credit, and debt work.

10. **Invest for retirement**—Learn about different approaches and their risks, select the best approach for you, and actively begin saving and investing for retirement. Don't wait! Starting now helps to ensure your secure retirement.

Working and saving aren't the only things in life. Somewhere along the way, you'll probably meet someone you want to spend your life with. This topic brings us to the next life phase on your journey toward the healthy, happy retirement you've begun to envision. Ready to see how life in a marriage or partnership could impact your retirement goals? Let's do it.

3

Marriage and Partners: Time to Double Down on Your Retirement Savings

RECENTLY, OUR FRIEND LINDA came to us in tears because her marriage had disintegrated. We were shocked. Everyone in our circle thought they were the perfect couple, with great kids and an incredible home in the Chicago suburbs. Matthew is a fire commissioner, and Linda is an international flight attendant. They always seemed so affectionate together.

"Out of nowhere he came home, quietly packed his suitcases, and calmly announced he was leaving," Linda sobbed. "I feel like this is a bad dream. How did this happen?"

Soon, a hidden backstory came to light: Matthew had been having an affair for years. He had been secretly unsatisfied in the marriage for a long time, he said, although he had never shared those feelings.

Now, as Linda deals with the emotional fallout and heads toward an ugly divorce, both partners are experiencing a steep slide in their financial security and their hopes for a well-off retirement. They've also lost friends who wanted to stay neutral through the divorce process, so their retirement could potentially be lonelier, too.

Many relationship breakups can be avoided with thoughtful partner selection and ongoing communication about values and life goals. The best time to have these important conversations is early on—before problems have a chance to fester.

Approach partnering with your eyes wide open. A breakup later in life can derail your retirement plan and set you back financially, emotionally, and logistically. This chapter is here to help you build a strong, lasting relationship—and avoid the kind of split that can send you sliding down the chute to square one, with worries of an uncertain future and insecure retirement.

Who you choose as a life partner is one of the most important decisions you'll ever make. Beyond physical attraction, are you truly compatible? Can your relationship go the distance?

When Fewer Choose Marriage

Today, between the trends toward marrying later in life and staying single by choice, just over half of marriageable-age Americans are married compared with two-thirds back in 1960, according to a 2024 US Census Bureau report. (If pairing up isn't for you, skip ahead to the next chapter—it covers the retirement journey for singles.)

More couples live together now, with more than one in ten couples sharing a home without tying the knot. In fact, our research led us to a 2023 Kiplinger article with this surprising finding: More young adults—two in five—say they think marriage is an outdated tradition!

Why not get married? It may feel less necessary to some of us, particularly women. In the past, women had far less financial power and were heavily reliant on a spouse's income. Until 1974, women couldn't get a credit card or buy a car without their husbands' help.

Now that more women work and have access to credit, some feel less need to marry. Also, many people who've had a previous marriage end in divorce swear they'll never take the plunge again.

Whether or not you and your partner legally tie the knot, it's important to know how your shared values, health habits, approach to planning, and financial attitudes will build a secure foundation for a lasting relationship. You should know the impact remaining unmarried can have on your retirement plan, too.

As a young, single person, you've had the chance to explore your own values, get healthy, learn about finance, build planning skills, and start saving for retirement. Now, it's time to compare notes with your new partner to see if you share a vision for the future. Let's start with the bedrock of all relationships—your values.

Share What Matters Most

Ah, the blush of first love! All you think about all day long is your partner's eyes, their lips, their body, their brilliant ideas, their sense of humor.

Too often, lovestruck couples don't discuss what's truly important in a budding relationship—whether their values align—or if there's even a workable compromise if they find that their values don't completely align. Instead of putting off the big talk about what you want out of life, let your values be your guide as you begin a relationship with a possible life partner.

Does your partner hold values that are radically different from your own? If so, resist the temptation to believe you'll change that person over time. As Tracy often says, bad habits rarely improve with age, and people don't change—they adjust. Take your partner at face value and accept who they are today, not who you hope they'll become. Then ask yourself honestly: Is this the person I want to share my life with, just as they are?

We learned about this sad story of a record-short marriage through our family grapevine.

———— ☕ ————

One of our younger friends was married for just three months. He was raised in a fundamentalist Christian family. Shortly after college, he met an attractive young woman at church.

Soon, they were totally smitten with each other. Everyone in their circle agreed they made a beautiful couple, and their parents were ecstatic. After a short courtship, they got married. But then the marriage ended before you could say Jack Robinson, shocking his religious community.

What happened? This couple turned out to have very different values.

Post-honeymoon, this young man explained to his bride that he wanted to raise his children strictly according to his faith's principles. Their children should be homeschooled or attend a nearby church school. Also, he wanted to have many children and didn't believe in birth control.

Perhaps he thought the fact that he'd graduated from a Christian college and they'd met at church made these values obvious.

But she didn't get the message before they tied the knot. And while she is a Christian, this wasn't her flavor. Once the new bride got the full rundown, they decided to part ways. Since they couldn't agree on these fundamental issues, it was probably smart to end this relationship sooner rather than later.

As this heartbreaking tale illustrates, you can save yourself so much grief by discussing core values early. Key values questions to ask your partner include:

- What kind of life do you see yourself living in five years?
- Is it like the kind of life I want to live, or is it totally different?
- Do our core values align? If not how different are they?
- If we have different values, can we find a compromise?
- What are your religious preferences?
- Do you want children or not?
- If you do want children, what kind of parent do you want to be? How involved would you be in raising, guiding, and disciplining the children?

If you want to travel constantly or live on a boat but your partner has to be dragged out of the house just to go to the neighborhood restaurant, you've got a problem. Likewise, if you don't own a television while theirs is never off, you may not be a match. Ask your partner if they would relocate for your job or if they never want to move away from your hometown. Discuss who's expected to do the housework. (So many fights are about this!)

Partnerships thrive when you ask these questions and shed light on each other's values, ensuring no big surprises are hiding out of sight. And knowing each other's values helps you pull together if your relationship hits rough seas. Love does not conquer all.

Identify Your Top Partner Traits

What are the values you seek in a partner? List the traits you most want in a partner. They could include personality traits, such as:

- Respectful
- Committed
- Loyal
- Clear communicator
- Forgiving
- Kind
- Honest
- Family focused
- Shares your faith (or lack of interest in religion)
- Shares your political views
- Takes good care of themselves
- Treats their parents well
- Has strong friendships
- Wants to live where you do

See if you can boil down your list to a top ten list of key values. After a date, you can review your list to see how well this person matches your values. When you meet someone whose values align with yours, it truly can feel like a match made in heaven. Finding "the one," a partner who shares your values, is a wonderful ladder to a better life.

Be sure to include one particular make-or-break value since you'll want to be on the same page—whether you want to become parents together. People tend to bend their values for their partner, and we know that compromise is essential to relationships, but this is one of those issues where you really shouldn't bend if you have a strong opinion on the matter.

The Kid Convo

Maybe you don't know how you feel about becoming a parent, but if you're getting into a serious relationship, it's time to figure it out. This is a sensitive area that breaks many relationships. Down the road, if one partner resents being saddled with unwanted children or resents missing out on their chance to be a parent, your relationship will be in jeopardy.

Do you want kids at all? Does your partner? How many? When? The answers may change over time, but it's important to have a baseline conversation in case one of you is strongly committed to a child-free life and one of you envisions having enough kids for a football team.

Would you rather start a family right away or delay having children, even if it could require expensive fertility treatments later? How do you feel about adoption? Given your jobs and income levels, will you be able to afford having a child or more than one? What support do you have for childrearing among your family, friends, and community?

If you get an answer you don't like during your kid convo, *believe it*. Don't think, "Oh, I'll change my partner's mind later."

With more people marrying later and remarrying, one or both partners may already have children and may not be interested in having more. One of you may not be able to have biological children. If you wait to share your excitement about having kids only to find out your new love has had a vasectomy or tubal ligation, with no wish to reverse the procedure, you've wasted precious time and energy on a dead-end relationship.

The decision about whether to become a parent is one of the most complex and fraught in our modern age. It's no surprise that an increasing number of reproductive-age Americans say they don't plan to have children, according to a 2021 Pew Research Center report.

Either way, your decision about whether to have kids ties into your retirement planning:

1. Kids are costly to raise and educate, so this can mean less money saved for retirement, but your children could support you in old age.

2. You could save more if you don't have children, but then it's up to you to secure your retirement, including caretaking in your elder years.

No matter what you decide, taking care of your health as you age is vitally important. This is the next aspect of marriage and partnering to consider.

In Sickness and In Health

If you find a partner when you're young, it's hard to imagine you'll ever become seriously ill. You feel invincible and immortal. But it's an illusion. Someday, someone in your relationship will get sick. A shared focus on staying healthy will help preserve both your relationship and your shot at a wealthy retirement.

One of the top ways to stay healthy is to stay insured and use all available preventive healthcare checkups. If you're laid off, extend your employer's health insurance benefits through COBRA or self-insure using your state's online insurance marketplace. Keep your healthcare access no matter what.

Note that spouses can be covered under their partner's health insurance policy, but your unmarried partner can't be covered. It's one of the reasons why gay people fought for the right to marry—so their partners can be covered on their health insurance.

If you're not married and want decision-making rights in case your partner is incapacitated, get a durable power of attorney for healthcare. That gives you access to your partner's medical records and the ability to make medical decisions for them if they can't.

A joint focus on staying healthy will help your partnership last. And it will help your savings last, given the direct connection between health and your financial future. A major health crisis can send you into a spiral of medical debt, and down the financial chute you go.

As we dug into the data on the Peterson-KFF Health System Tracker, we learned the majority of people grappling with medical debt are in poor health. Avoid

this sinkhole and encourage each other to take care of yourselves, which will help keep your retirement plan on track. Taking care of yourself begins with keeping your body moving.

Couples Who Sweat Together Stay Together

It's no secret that shared activities help keep relationships healthy. While we knew this intuitively, we found various articles in our research that supported this point, including an appropriately titled article in *Psychology Today*: "The Importance of Shared Interests in Relationships."

To keep your bodies healthy, some of those shared activities should involve exercise. If all the activities you have in common involve sitting—especially in bars—you may not live long enough to enjoy those golden years. Despite clear links between exercise and health, nearly one-third of adults face high risks, such as heart disease and diabetes, due to a sedentary lifestyle.

Staying active is hugely important for lifetime health, and having shared activities is great for your relationship. So, finding ways to work out together is always a win while pursuing some favorite activities for yourself as well. For example, we both love hiking, bicycling, skiing, and more. We love the outdoors and being together, while Tracy's exercise regimen also includes weight training and other gym-based workouts.

A couple's health is also shaped by what they regularly eat together.

You Are What You . . .

Couples who prioritize eating healthy meals together build a strong foundation for a vibrant, active retirement. Of course, each partner brings their own food preferences and long-standing habits to the table—literally.

When you were single, no one blinked if dinner meant greasy take-out tacos or eating straight from the package while standing at the kitchen counter. But in a partnership, food becomes a shared experience—you're shopping, cooking, and eating together. You may have strong ideas about family meals. For example, you may insist on eating dinner together every evening, while your partner may only be able to share a dinnertime meal a few days a week due to work, volunteer, or family obligations. So, what happens when your habits collide?

While some couples eat healthily without much effort (perhaps thanks to their upbringing), most of us must be intentional about our eating habits. Ideally, your relationship becomes a source of support, not sabotage, when it comes to nourishing your bodies.

Yes, we're in an era that opposes a weight-focused culture—and rightly so. We're entirely on board with the body positivity movement, which encourages self-love and respect at any size. That said, loving yourself also means taking care of yourself in the present and looking ahead to the future. Where are your current eating and exercise habits taking you? It's not about chasing a number on the scale but protecting your long-term health. Heart disease, diabetes, strokes, and other preventable conditions claim far too many lives. Let's focus on habits that help you thrive today and in the decades to come.

Will Your Partner Be a Caregiver? Three Clues

If you think serious illness or disability is only a worry for the very elderly, here's a wake-up call: The CDC reports that the vast majority of adults over age fifty-five have at least one chronic condition.

You can ask someone you're dating if they'll still need you, if they'll still feed you when you're sixty-four, but you'll only get a theoretical answer. But you can find clues to your partner's future caregiving skills. Look at how they treat their parents and other relatives who need help when they are ill or scheduled for surgery or working to overcome a physical challenge. Here are three questions to ask yourself:

1. **Do they volunteer?** Notice if they volunteer to drive friends and family to doctors' appointments or if they shrink away from sick people's needs.

2. **Do they visit?** When they hear someone is ill, watch to see if they disappear until that person is well again or if they deliver a meal and stay to offer some words of comfort.

3. **Do they step up?** When you're down with the flu, do they head to the store for more Tylenol and pick up the slack on your chores without being asked?

Observe your partner's current behavior around sick people or others in need. This is how they'll treat you if you have a major illness or disability down the road. Find a caring partner, and you'll be glad later. If there's a large age gap between you, the younger one should plan for how they'll care for their older partner, who'll likely have issues first. As a case in point, Chris shares this conversation with a friend.

———————— ☕ ————————

Recently, I raised this question with my friend, Bill, who's forty, and his unmarried partner of fifteen years, Georgia, is fifty-five. "Are you prepared to take care of her when she's seventy-five and you're sixty?" I asked Bill. "Could you live off one income when she can no longer work?"

The short answer was no. Georgia had always been the higher earner, and Bill wasn't clear about how he would take on the financial and caregiving challenges. Like most people his age, he thinks this kind of care is a long way off.

My advice? I suggested that Georgia look into long-term care insurance for herself, which might fill the gap. This is one of those important issues they should have talked about early on, but they are talking about it now and putting plans in place.

———————————————

With a bit of prompting, Bill and Georgia realized an important issue was lurking in the background of their relationship. Talking about this issue brought it to the surface, so together, they could discuss their thoughts and fears and put a plan in place. Being able to talk about your innermost thoughts and fears is vital to a successful partnership. Let's explore this point a bit more.

Unpack Your Bags

When you jump into a new relationship without processing why the old ones ended, it spells trouble for your new romance. Here's an example:

We were there to support our friend, Marty, when his wife passed away after more than fifty years of marriage. In his grief, he felt lonely and wanted to be in a relationship. Instead of sorting out his emotional baggage first, he met Sally and remarried within a few years.

Sally was from a completely different background and culture than our native-born American friend. As they settled into married life together, Marty was surprised to learn she planned to continue running her business, which took her away from many of the household tasks his late wife generally took care of. He assumed Sally would provide the same level of care and attention to him and their household.

"I'd miss my customers, and I want my own income," she told him. "Family is also very important to me, and I need time to take care of my elderly parents. In our culture this is very important."

In their rush to marry, neither of them asked questions to ensure their personal core values aligned. They never had that important conversation about what they expected of each other. This is where sharing values early in your relationship comes in handy at every age as well as unpacking your emotional baggage. In Marty's case, much of his emotional baggage was tied to his underlying grief and loneliness as well as a false belief that his next relationship would be similar to or even a continuation of his previous relationship.

Luckily, they sat down and had "the values talk" before making any sudden changes, and each agreed to be there for events and activities, such as holidays and supporting each other's hobbies and family needs. Marty agreed to help with *her business and with household chores and meals, so they both would feel taken care of. Now, he's optimistic they can make their marriage work. But they would have had a less rocky start if they'd had this talk when they first met.*

———————————————

Whether you meet your partner at nineteen or forty-nine, you've lived a life before this moment. Some experiences may have been wonderful, but most of us acquire some emotional scars as we travel through life.

When you drag unresolved emotional baggage into a new partnership, it casts a shadow over your new happiness that can destroy your relationship. It's time to crack open that suitcase and start unpacking the emotional baggage you've long ignored.

Whatever the cause of your trauma, the first step is to be honest. Are you haunted by past events you've been afraid to face? Do you find yourself overreacting or having inappropriate responses to relatively innocuous actions or comments in this relationship?

If so, it's time to seek help. You need to get these old hurts out in the open, so you can work through them and finally let them go. There's no excuse for not dealing with emotional baggage today. If you can't find a therapist or in-person support group in your town that's a fit, you can investigate numerous online support groups, virtual workshops, and more.

How can you make sure your emotional baggage doesn't doom your current relationship? You may find your baggage scary or embarrassing to talk about, we know. But buck up your courage, and be transparent about your life and how past events have affected you. It's the first step to building a strong relationship.

If you're self-aware, have a good EQ, and have a solid idea of your values, you'll be open with your partner. We have faith in you.

Later on, if something happens that makes you uncomfortable, talk about it right away. Don't toss it in your suitcase and start accumulating new baggage. We are big advocates of developing and practicing good communications skills. Learn what these are and utilize them regularly.

Why is this important for your retirement plan? If your relationships keep falling apart due to your habit of stuffing your baggage under the bed—decade after decade—it endangers the foundation you're trying to build for a financially comfortable retirement. It's simple math: The older you are when you find your life partner, the fewer years you will have to pool your resources and save for a secure retirement.

When you start a new relationship with someone you feel you could share your life with, someone who shares your values and life goals, do it in the best way possible. Be honest about who you are and what you need from your partner. Learn how to communicate your needs and be open to those of your partner.

The Financial Perks of Togetherness

Many couples daydream together about their life plans— the great city they want to move to, their shining career paths, and how many kids they want.

Far fewer couples discuss how pooling their finances would make those dreams come true. If you both work, you have more money coming in. Can this double income help you achieve the life you want?

Your retirement planning process has some unique aspects if you're married versus not married. Most married couples open joint savings accounts, and unmarried partners generally do not. Unmarried partners may even maintain two homes, an extra expense that makes it harder to save.

If you are not married and buy a home together, treat it as the investment it is. Be clear about the financial responsibilities for each of you, and make sure you legally define your ownership stake. If this relationship ends, you'll be glad you protected yourself and can walk away with your share of the profits.

> **BIG TIP:** Sharing your resources to cut expenses and save money is a proven way to build wealth.

The other key ingredient for retirement planning? Openly sharing your finances.

Where Are You Now?

To start, take a look at the assets and debts for both of you and ask yourselves these questions:

- Do either of you have money saved, or do you own property?
- If you have student loans, car loans, or credit card debt, what are the payoff timelines?
- Could you pay off any of these now?
- Are you living within your means or not?

Know where you both are right now financially. To start saving, you may need to slash expenses or get a side hustle going. Whatever you do, don't delegate money issues to one half of your pair. It's a job for both of you.

When Ignorance Is Not Bliss

In our experience, many people—most of them women—let their partner handle the finances. When half the couple is in the dark about money, it creates a culture of secrecy.

When this happens, racking up debt on a credit card your partner doesn't know about seems more acceptable. Or getting a second mortgage in your name only. You're deceiving your partner and undermining your relationship. Sooner or later, your secret money moves will come to light, and your partner will feel betrayed. It's a common relationship killer.

As an acquaintance found out, choosing financial ignorance can have tragic consequences.

———————— ☕ ————————

Jennifer married a financial officer for a big corporation. Like many women, she let him handle all their family finances. For instance, she never questioned it when Edward refinanced their home after a long European family trip.

"He knows so much more than I do about managing money," she explained. At tax time, she blithely signed their joint tax forms without reading them.

When their daughter reached high school, Jennifer was surprised to learn there was no college fund for her education. Eventually, due to finding even more discrepancies in their finances along with too many discussions about his alcohol use, she asked him for a divorce. Unfortunately, she didn't know how much money they had or where it was.

"How do you know what he owes you in the divorce?" we asked.

"I'm trusting him," Jennifer replied.

Who knows what fortune of retirement money this high-earning spouse hid from her? Unfortunately, the responsibility for this family's financial troubles falls partially on her because she never participated in their financial decisions and was blissfully in the dark.

If you don't understand what's going on with your money, ask questions. Make it clear you want to be part of all major financial decisions regardless of whether you are working or not. You are in a partnership. Commit to financial honesty and transparency. There should be no hidden money.

Discuss your financial future: Will you both keep working? Will one of you stay home with your children for a time? Will one or both of you retire early? These are questions to navigate together from the beginning.

In addition, each of you should be involved with tax preparation and know how much you're paying in taxes. It's helpful to know that US tax laws view married couples and unmarried partners differently.

Four Marriage Money Advantages

Yes, taxes are unromantic but also unavoidable. Being legally married gives you an edge in this aspect of your relationship. Here are a few benefits we uncovered in our research:

1. Married couples can give each other unlimited money during their lifetimes, but unmarried couples need to track and limit these annually to avoid gift taxes.

2. A spouse who doesn't work can contribute to their IRA using the working spouse's income. This can double a couple's retirement deposits.

3. Married couples filing jointly generally pay less federal income tax than unmarried partners.

4. You can leave unlimited amounts of money to your spouse through an estate plan, and they'll pay zero tax.

We're not saying "get married for the tax breaks," but you should be aware of the tax consequences of staying unmarried. Keep your finger on the pulse of the various tax advantages and consequences—including the four we mentioned above—since they can change whenever tax laws change. Your best resources are the IRS website and your accountant.

A recent conversation Chris had with a longtime friend illustrates the problem of not being aware of the tax consequences of your partnership.

———————— ☕ ————————

Our sixty-six-year-old friend, Andy, remarried twenty years ago. It was a second marriage for both him and his new bride, June. They were so happy to find each other that they rushed into marriage without having a conversation about their values or their finances. He moved to her family home in New England as he'd lost his house in the divorce, but otherwise they kept their finances separate.

Andy and June both enjoyed successful professional careers and had their own incomes. Since both had come out on the short end financially in their divorces, they were leery of mixing their finances.

The years ticked by, and they never reevaluated the decision to remain "financially single." They even filed separate taxes every year, which robbed them of cash they could have invested. June earned more money than Andy, but because they viewed themselves as financially independent and never discussed opportunities to cooperatively invest, they never used some of her income to increase his IRA deposits. In fact, they never pursued any shared financial planning whatsoever.

When more costs came along, it created a financial crisis for this couple. We'll pick up Andy and June's story in the next chapter.

Our friend was technically married but financially functioned like a single man, which resulted in lost opportunities to save for retirement, create an emergency fund, pay less taxes every year, and plan for a secure future for him and his family. Meanwhile, other couples are in the opposite situation—they haven't legally married but assume they have marital status.

Do you think you have a common-law marriage because you've lived together for more than seven years? Do a little research. Only a handful of states recognize common-law marriage as being legally equivalent to more formal, legally recognized marriages and give those partners the same tax, gift, and inheritance rights. These states have very specific requirements to prove the existence of your common-law marriage.

Besides the tax disadvantages, unmarried couples may have a harder time qualifying for a mortgage or other loan as bankers view these couples as a riskier bet. Their viewpoint is backed by the fact that more than half of unmarried couples will split up, while only one-third will get married, according to the Institute for Family Studies.

If you haven't tied the knot, have a chat with your partner about whether you want to reconsider.

Now, let's turn our attention to specific steps you can take to start planning your financial future together.

A Monthly Joint Project

Creating a household budget for two is an important step toward building a solid financial foundation for your life together.

If you're planning an expensive wedding or lavish honeymoon, your budgeting efforts should start before you walk down the aisle. A 2024 article in *Forbes* magazine found that the average cost of a wedding has soared to more than $30,000. So, if your parents aren't footing the bill, you could start your union saddled with quite a large debt, which might take years to pay off.

———————— ☕ ————————

A couple we know offered their son $40,000 toward his wedding, or he and his fiancé could put the money toward a home down payment instead. The couple chose to apply the money toward a down payment and bought a small starter home in an up-and-coming suburb in Virginia. The young couple enjoyed a modest wedding and are building wealth by owning property.

Instead of setting up a registry and asking for knick-knacks you may not need, consider creating a wedding or honeymoon fund where well-wishers can contribute cash. Living within your means as a couple should start on day one.

As we mentioned, creating a budget should start before you tie the knot. Once married, commit to teaming up together to update your monthly budget. Grab all your recent monthly statements and sort your expenses into categories. You can find plenty of free, online tools to help you streamline this process.

Charting every single expenditure can be quite an eye-opener. Now, you have real data on how much you earn and how much you spend on various types of purchases and activities. That means you can ask yourselves some important questions:

- What is our monthly income?

- What are our fixed monthly expenses, such as groceries, utilities, and rent or mortgage?

- What do we expect to pay in taxes?

- After these basic expenses, how much can we save for our emergency fund and for retirement?

- How much do we have left for discretionary spending—eating out, travel, entertainment, clothing, and so forth?

Now that you have this info, you can discuss your spending habits as individuals and as a couple. Are you naturally frugal, or are you spending all your money the weekend after you get your paycheck? Not to indulge in stereotypes, but are you a man who buys toys or a woman who relies on "retail therapy" to cheer herself up?

We're not here to judge—just be aware of how much run room you have for discretionary purchases before you get into debt. If you both need to stop buying daily lattes or whatever's marketed to you on social media, commit to making those cutbacks together.

Next, find ways to reduce spending. Hunt and kill any recurring subscriptions you've forgotten about. You can check your credit and debit card statements or use a subscription management app like Recurly or Rocket Money to help you find and cancel subscriptions.

Examine the rest of your purchases. Is everything a great value? Do you get joy from it? If not, maybe you can find some easy cutbacks.

Most Americans live beyond their means by amassing significant revolving credit card debt and making minimum payments. Collectively, we have over $1 trillion racked up on our credit cards, an average of more than $6,000 each. (These dollar amounts are from a 2024 CNBC article and, chances are, will grow higher every year.) Having that much high-interest debt is like playing our Chutes and Ladders game with a very long chute leading down into a very deep hole.

If you and your partner want a secure retirement, don't fall into this financial pit. Commit to spending less than you earn each month while saving as much as you can for retirement. Don't believe us? Ask a financial advisor.

Yes, You Can Get Help

If you're barely squeaking by each month on what you earn, it may sound crazy to seek professional financial advice. But early guidance has many benefits. Seek out a qualified financial advisor who has recently set up shop or an acquaintance who might give you a free consultation.

When you meet, assess the fit. See whether you and your partner feel comfortable sharing your financial details and asking questions. If not, keep looking.

You want to work with an accredited, licensed financial advisor. Take the time to check the credentials to avoid falling into the hands of a scammer. If you've made a budget and have saved even $1,000, a financial planner can look at your budget and make suggestions to help you cut some expenses, commit to saving more, and invest that grand as seed money in your retirement fund.

More importantly, a planner can help you connect your current life to retirement down the road. As we mentioned, retirement may seem like a million years away, but actively visualizing and planning your retirement will inspire you to more aggressively save for retirement. Your financial advisor can also answer questions, such as:

- How much will we need to save to have the kind of retirement we want?

- Are we saving enough monthly to reach that goal now, or do we need to accelerate our savings plan?

A financial advisor can help you and your partner create a savings plan that gets you to your retirement goal.

If you're living frugally but your living expenses exceed your income, it's time to brainstorm how to earn more. Could one of you ask for a raise or change jobs to one with higher pay? Maybe you could sell items on eBay. If you have a big place, perhaps you could rent out a spare room or consider moving to more modest digs.

Apply your values here, too. Do you have similar views on the importance of saving money and living frugally? Find a compromise if you need to, but get on the same page.

Whatever your choices, you will likely achieve your vibrant, rewarding, and secure retirement through some sacrifice, giving up some instant gratification to build wealth for your later years. It's up to the two of you to decide what you're both willing to give up, so you can achieve the retirement you envision. Set a savings goal you can both live with, and review this monthly to see if you're staying on track. Otherwise, vows to save more tend to go by the wayside over time.

Once you develop a regular habit of saving money as a couple, it's time to learn about investing. To end up with a fat retirement account, you'll need to know how to invest your money to make it grow over time.

How to Start Investing

Now that you have some savings, you should choose how to grow your money. It's time to figure out your risk tolerance as a couple and select retirement investments that will bring in more than a high-yield savings account.

Don't put this off. Remember, the longer your money has to grow, the easier it is to retire rich. You also have more time to recover from any investment setbacks, such as a stock market slump or a period of low interest rates that slows your growth. The first step is to decide the type of investments you're comfortable with and which ones feel out of bounds for you.

Find Your Approach

Our attitudes about investing tend to be shaped by what we saw our parents and other family members do. Maybe they bought and rented out apartments and did well, or perhaps they put all their faith in their company's stock plan and then the corporation went bust. You may want to avoid strategies relatives and friends used or mimic their approach, depending on their results. Don't limit your knowledge to personal experience, though. Learn about the different types of investing and the levels of risk they carry.

Let's start with diversification. Put simply, don't put all your eggs in one basket. If you're buying stocks, don't put all your money in one security. Also, buy something else that tends to go up when stocks go down, such as bonds.

If you have a corporate job, take a serious look at what the company's 401(k) plan offers. Usually, these plans include a limited number of mutual funds and other basic options and some guidance on staying diversified. If you don't understand the choices, ask the HR department about learning opportunities.

If your company's 401(k) offers a matching contribution, take it. You want every dollar of that free money. It's basically a no-cost ladder to more savings. Too bad that over 40 percent of American workers with access to a 401(k) plan don't use it, according to a 2023 CNBC survey.

If you can save more and want to explore taking more risk, you could put another chunk in a brokerage account where you have more investing choices.

The question of how to invest is another area where your financial advisor can provide education. Plus, you can find plenty of basic investing information online to further your education. Seek out trusted sources, such as the basics guide from FINRA, the Financial Industry Regulatory Authority.

Maybe one of you is drawn to more volatile investments, such as buying precious metals or day-trading individual stocks. Meanwhile, your partner may be too nervous about stock market investing to even buy mutual funds or exchange-traded funds (ETFs), two types of stocks that lower your risk by owning many different securities. That more anxious partner may prefer to invest in municipal bonds or high-yield savings accounts that pay a guaranteed interest rate and focus on simply storing more away.

How much risk feels right to each of you? You may need to meet in the middle by investing some of your money conservatively and some in more speculative ventures. Your financial advisor can guide you to identify your risk tolerances and find a middle ground that is not too conservative or too aggressive since either strategy could risk your goal of enjoying a secure retirement.

Insure Your Success

Does choosing investments feel overwhelming? There's definitely a lot to learn. If the two of you can't agree on an investment strategy, don't have time to learn about it right now, or you're just risk averse, let's talk about another conservative way to save—through life insurance.

What does life insurance have to do with retirement? When you choose a policy, whether it is a permanent, whole life, or universal policy (depending on what's right for you), you can carry a cash value that grows as you pay premiums over time. You can later borrow or "cash out" that money while you're still alive.

This kind of life insurance can earn guaranteed returns without having to become a financial whiz. The insurance company's professional investment managers make sure your deposited premiums grow, and you don't have to think about it.

If you choose the insurance route, work with a certified professional who takes the time to understand your needs and tailor the right coverage for you and your family. And don't forget to review and update your beneficiaries regularly. Why? Because couples don't always stay together.

For some people, their 401(k) can bring the same or a higher yield in savings or a CD, so remember to ask questions and work with a Certified Financial Planner (CFP)® for answers.

Breakup Prevention: Why It Matters

As the song says, breaking up is hard to do. A breakup can bring heartache and significant life disruption. What the song *doesn't* say is that ending your relationship is commonly a financial disaster—especially for women. When it comes to divvying up the dough, divorce laws tend to favor the main breadwinner, who is usually male. So, women most often emerge from a divorce substantially poorer, while men may see a smaller decline or even a slight uptick in their financial fortunes, as reported by the National Library of Medicine.

Divorce can create a massive chute that endangers your retirement plan. How common is divorce? The stats are a bit tricky as most studies track divorces in a single year and don't follow couples throughout their relationship. But our research shows a general drift of nearly half of American marriages ending in divorce. Over the past twenty years or so, the divorce rate has declined, but it's still awfully high, and the divorce rate is even higher for second marriages.

Why do couples divorce? The number one cause is disagreements about money, according to multiple reports. This is a big reason why it's important to commit to transparency around finances. Other common reasons include:

- Cheating
- Lack of intimacy or closeness
- Doesn't feel like a partnership

You should be able to avoid all these problems if you're in a relationship where you have shared values, are in touch with your feelings, have unpacked your emotional baggage, and communicate honestly and openly with your partner.

It's our great hope that you can use the ideas in this book to avoid the emotional and financial sinkhole of divorce. Yes, some marriages need to end—perhaps physical or verbal abuse, substance abuse, or mental-health problems make it extremely challenging or even unsafe for a partner to stay. But if there's any way you can work it out, pause before you run to the courthouse and file divorce papers. Avoid a knee-jerk or instant divorce because of one problem or incident. This is a major decision that will impact the rest of your life on every level. So, take it slow.

Had a spat? Give yourselves time to cool off and talk it through. Besides salvaging your relationship, you might literally save a fortune. If you're older and contemplating divorce, that advice goes double.

The Perils of "Gray Divorce"

We've talked about the trend toward getting married later. Unfortunately, we're seeing an additional, more disturbing trend. Our research revealed that twice as many people are now divorcing after age fifty as in the 1990s.

The so-called gray divorce has a grave financial impact. Unlike couples who split up in their twenties or thirties, a fifty-five-year-old has much less time to earn more and rebuild their retirement account.

Gray divorce hits women the hardest. A Pew Research Center study found that their earnings tend to be lower due to wage sexism and employment gaps to stay home with kids. That means most women's ability to jump back into the workforce and earn well isn't as good as their male counterparts. And a Prudential report revealed that women typically have less saved for retirement, so they have more ground to make up.

How big is the gender gap in gray divorce? An analysis of a decade of economic data, published in a 2022 *Forbes* magazine article, revealed that women divorcing after age fifty saw an average 45 percent drop in their standard of living. By contrast, divorced men' s lifestyles shrank less than half that much.

One recent personal experience brought home to Chris how important it is for older couples to fight for their marriages.

My longtime friend, Sam, and I met for lunch at the local diner. When he arrived, the seventy-year-old plopped into our booth's red, upholstered seat and proclaimed that he and his spouse, Nancy, were feuding and had decided to divorce—after fifty years of marriage.

"I've moved out," he told me. "I can't put up with her anymore!"

I asked him, "Why are you getting divorced now? Is one of you seeing someone else?"

"No," he said. "I've just had it!"

While we waited for our sandwiches, I asked if he'd thought about the financial impact for both of them by divorcing this late in life.

"You'd have to set up and pay for two households, and that's only the beginning of the additional costs," I told him.

If one of them fell ill or became disabled, I explained, they would be alone and would need to hire a caregiver. Their odds of ending up in costly assisted living would skyrocket. Also, Nancy was receiving health benefits as his spouse—vital support that she'd lose if they divorced.

After our lunch, Sam and Nancy had a long talk. Reality hit. Her health is already failing, and they concluded it wasn't worth the financial downside to get divorced. After meeting with a financial advisor, they decided to sell their home and split the proceeds. They plan to live separate lives without divorcing, which will preserve the health benefits Nancy needs.

If you want to avoid starting over financially, especially later in life, your best option is to find a way to stay married. Barring that, you could also explore a legal separation. Here are a few key takeaways about legal separation:

- It's a court-ordered agreement where a married couple usually lives apart.

- The separation court order may specify financial obligations, child custody and visitation agreements, and child support.

- A legal separation is preferred over divorce by some people for religious or financial reasons or because they have young children.

- Separated spouses may be entitled to certain benefits as married couples. Of course, you would need to consult with an attorney to know your rights and options.

If you're thinking your relationship can't be saved, you need a departure plan.

Plan Before You Leap

Our friend Natalie saved her financial life and ensured a secure retirement by carefully planning her departure from a controlling and unfaithful spouse.

———————— ☕ ————————

Natalie took a year to plan her exit from an unhealthy marriage. Brett was a successful lawyer, and Natalie was a well-respected interior designer, and they lived in a Manhattan penthouse. She suspected he was cheating, and when she knew for sure she consulted a lawyer about her options. Armed with knowledge of her rights, she quietly separated her own finances and purchased a place to live in her own name. She had everything ready and waiting for the day she would decide it was time to leave.

She knew Brett can be emotionally abusive and might try to gaslight her into staying. Having an escape plan in place gave Natalie peace of mind that, when she was ready, she could make a clean break with her own money intact. In other words, she carefully packed a parachute before jumping out of the plane. Too many people don't look before they leap from a split, with tragic consequences for their finances, freedom, and secure retirement.

We're pleased to share that Natalie successfully made her "jump out of the plane." She is enjoying this chapter of life in her new home—and enjoying financial security—thanks to the fact that she carefully packed her parachute!

Hopefully, you won't need to make this kind of plan. You've chosen a compatible partner by vetting your common values early on, unpacking your emotional baggage, enjoying open and honest communication, and committing to financial transparency with each other.

When Unmarried Partners Split

What if you're not married when your relationship comes to an end? The emotional outcome may be just as intense, but the financial result can be different and more complicated.

How you divide your assets depends on whether you kept your finances separate or combined them and whether you're in a community property state. If you bought a home in both your names and opened a joint bank account, your finances are commingled.

> **BIG TIP:** Put your financial arrangement in writing early in your relationship to ensure who owns what is clear in case you break up. Otherwise, you may have made all the mortgage payments on your own, but legally half of your house could belong to your partner in a split.

If you are a partner hoping for alimony, we have bad news: Usually, neither partner is entitled to alimony payments without a previously written agreement. This is yet another reason why women should consider marriage since they're more likely to seek alimony.

Top Nine Takeaways for Couples

With over half of marriages ending in divorce, you must be proactive at every step in your relationship, starting from the beginning. This chapter's key points should help:

1. **Define the values you want in a partner—** When you meet "the one" make sure you see them with clear eyes.

2. **Share your core values—**This is how you learn if you're truly compatible.

3. **Do you want marriage or not?**—Know the disadvantages of being in a partnership rather than a marriage.

4. **Discuss children early**—It's critical to make sure your desires are aligned.

5. **Build healthy habits together**—This strategy helps to ensure your partnership will endure, and you will enjoy a healthy, vibrant retirement together.

6. **Assess your partner as a caretaker**—Will they stick with you if you become seriously ill?

7. **Be honest about your emotional baggage**—Open and honest communication is vital, or you may sandbag your relationship.

8. **Commit to financial transparency**—Create your budget together, do all your financial and retirement planning together, and pay taxes together.

9. **Agree on an investing approach**—As a couple, seek help from a financial advisor and start growing your retirement funds.

Keep your relationship strong to avoid a split. Divorce can be an emotional and financial disaster that imperils your retirement goals. From here, you take on the challenging work of planning and saving for retirement alone. Welcome to the single life.

4

Saving as a Single for Your Secure Retirement

SOME PEOPLE MAY find themselves single one day through death or divorce, while many others are single by choice. This means, whether you are thirty or fifty, you need to create a rock-solid plan to ensure a secure retirement. This is the case with our friend, Brian.

———— ☕ ————

At fifty, Brian told us he doesn't see himself finding someone to settle down with. We suspect low self-esteem and past struggles navigating relationships may play a part. But the important thing to him is that he hasn't saved enough to take care of another person in his golden years.

He's a successful salesman in Michigan, but he has only saved enough for himself in his retirement account. If he met someone at this late date, they'd have to be able to support themself and fund their own retirement, or the relationship would be a no-go.

If you're single and expect to stay that way, it means you have to build your own ladder to the retirement you want, rung by rung.

As you know, we believe taking care of your health is an important rung on your ladder. This helps to ensure you'll enjoy good health in your golden years. Single people need to take care of their own physical and mental health and health insurance. Staying fit and eating healthily is up to you, with no partner on your case, reminding you to eat your broccoli, do your workouts, and take good care of yourself.

Planning the financial side of your single life is tricky because it's harder to build enough savings for a wealthy retirement on one income. Unfortunately, this challenge falls disproportionately on women.

This Is for All the Single Ladies

While this chapter is for anybody who's single, here's a simple fact: Women are living increasingly longer than men, according to an article in the November 2023 *Journal of the American Medical Association.* So, it's no surprise that single women outnumber men, with one hundred single women for every ninety single men, per a 2023 US Census Bureau report. This statistic tells us that many women who are currently single are likely to remain single because, as it turns out, there really aren't "plenty more fish in the sea."

Women also struggle to earn what they're worth. Women make an average of 82 cents to men's dollar for similar roles, a pay equity gap that has not changed meaningfully in the past twenty years. (This finding is presented in a 2023 article appropriately titled "The Enduring Grip of the Gender Pay Gap" by the Pew Research Center.)

And who takes care of ill children or elderly parents, often taking time off work and further limiting their income? The vast majority of caregivers are women.

To top it off, life can be more expensive when you're female. Women often pay more for products marketed to them than men pay for similar products packaged for males, a common pattern known as the *pink tax*.

How can singles—especially women—triumph over the odds to build a secure retirement? It starts with financial knowledge.

Single and Financially Savvy

When you're single, it's important to know how much money you have because it's *all* you have. Once you take stock of your savings, checking, and other assets, size up your debt. Are you living beyond your means? If so, your retirement hopes rest on making some cuts, figuring out how to earn more, or both.

Singles need a monthly budget just as much as couples do—maybe more. We already talked about couples cutting out the lattes and impulse buying. Well, in a household with only one income, that advice goes double. Figure out where your money is going, so you can decide if you need to change your spending habits—or your career. Here's a friend's career-change example.

Victoria, a long-divorced woman in her fifties, was barely making ends meet with her plant business, which served local restaurants. A longtime pet lover and owner of a beloved Weimaraner, she decided it was time to improve her situation. She returned to school to become a veterinary assistant.

Juggling work and school for several years was challenging, but it proved to be worth it. This career change doubled Victoria's hourly wage and allowed her to work more hours, significantly increasing her income and providing her with greater financial security. As a result, she and her fur baby were able to move from a tiny studio apartment to a larger apartment, and she established a solid financial foundation for her retirement.

Changing careers is just one way you can earn more. If you have a corporate job, take advantage of every available company perk, including the 401(k) and employer matching contribution. Maximize your benefits and figure out your risk tolerance, so you can invest your money for growth.

Starting a side business that could become a full-time endeavor is another way to improve your finances. It certainly did that for Chris. Business ownership also gives you tax write-offs you can really use as a single.

Another wealth builder for singles is to buy a house. If you can, do it sooner rather than later. If you don't have children, you have fewer expenses and can more readily save for a down payment. Riding the property-appreciation train is a proven way to build wealth, and the sooner you buy, the more likely you'll sell at a profit later.

Depending on your income level, you may qualify for a subsidized mortgage interest rate or other first-time buyer program. Some communities offer subsidies or below-market rate housing to people in specific careers, such as teaching, nursing, or first-responder roles. Investigate what's available locally when you're thinking about buying, both in terms of national incentives and local programs.

Once you earn more, you need to make that extra money grow. As we noted in previous chapters, find a trustworthy certified investment advisor who can give you good advice when you're getting started and guide you to ensure your investments grow over time. You can also learn about investing by joining a money club where you can hear others discuss their investment strategies, successes, and failures. Take the time to read about investment strategies, follow podcasts, and ask friends what they're doing. Whatever your approach, become a student of money management.

All these strategies—changing careers, maximizing corporate benefits, buying real estate, and smart investing—can really help when it's time to retire. It may seem impossible, but with careful planning and frugal living, singles can build the foundation for a secure retirement.

Five Money Tips for Singles

1. **Save for emergencies**—Sock away five to ten months of take-home pay in an FDIC- or NCUA-insured, high-yield savings account. Yes, that's more than the standard advice because there's only

one income in your household, which means more risk. Keep this fund separate from other savings, so you don't dip into it. Without an emergency fund, you're one incident away from a financial crisis.

2. **Know your spending**—Analyze your habits and stop overspending, especially if you're deficit-financing your lifestyle on credit cards. If you can't afford something you want, save for it or live without it. No more social media splurges!

3. **Learn smart money moves**—Find a financial mentor or certified financial advisor. Get trustworthy money advice to build the assets you need for your future. For instance, did you know that long-term investments are taxed at lower rates than short-term ones? You can always learn about money management no matter how little you have saved. Singles need to avoid high-risk investments even more than couples do since there's only one person's income to replace any lost capital.

4. **Get tax advice**—As a single, especially if you don't have children, you have fewer tax write-offs. So, get an accountant or financial advisor to walk you through the available tax-saving options.

5. **Create money goals for your future**—Besides retirement, what else do you want to do that will take serious cash? Maybe you're saving for a home or planning a big trip. If you don't have children, you may want to help with a niece or nephew's wedding or college tuition. If so, plan for those expenses, too. Create a separate savings account for each money goal and allot some available cash to each one monthly.

Know this—as a single, you can plan for and attain a healthy, wealthy retirement. Don't give up on your retirement dreams.

Top Seven Takeaways for Singles

Follow our tips to build your dream retirement solo:

1. **Women live longer**—This means many women are likely to end up single. Be prepared.

2. **Take care of your physical and mental health**—This is a critical component for a healthy, wealthy retirement.

3. **Learn to save and manage money**—You can build a nice retirement if you plan, budget, and stay focused on your retirement goal.

4. **Consider a more lucrative career**—You may need to switch careers to build wealth.

5. **Budget and live below your means**—This is how singles retire rich.

6. **Know your tax situation**—Singles pay more, so be sure to get professional tax advice.

7. **Set money goals**—Staying focused on your goals will help you stay disciplined about spending and saving, so you can create the retirement you envision.

Whether you're single or in a relationship, your retirement picture gets more complicated if you add children to the mix. We'll address this stage of life in the next chapter.

5

Having Children Changes Your Life— And Your Retirement Plan

THE DECISION TO become a parent is one of the most important ones you'll make, both emotionally and financially. Try not to jump into it without deep thought.

As a parent, life can be busy, and money can be tight. That goes double if you're a single parent. During your child-raising years, all the work you've done budgeting to save for retirement will be put to the test. Can you keep climbing the ladder you're on that leads to a healthy and wealthy retirement, or will you slide down a rung or two?

Adding a child or children to your household means you now have more family members to keep physically and emotionally healthy, which means more costs—all while staying true to your values and continuing to build your retirement nest egg. Whew!

If you and your spouse or partner are hoping to have children, here's a crazy idea: Plan ahead for it, just as you

would for any other long-term goal. A baby brings joy and a host of new expenses.

How can you prepare for all those new costs? Here are six tips:

1. Build a budget based on typical child-rearing costs to forecast your expenses.

2. Pay down or pay off high-interest accounts to cut interest fees.

3. Build an emergency fund with enough to cover three to six months of expenses.

4. Discuss childcare and education costs to set expectations.

5. Talk with grandparents about financial help they may be able to offer for a new grandchild.

6. Start a college savings fund or Roth IRA to help you save for education costs.

Plan ahead for the arrival of that bundle of joy if you can. Some kids arrive unexpectedly; perhaps you gain stepchildren in a second marriage. Either way, the child-raising years are one of the toughest stages when it comes to saving for retirement.

How many children you have also shapes your retirement journey. Having fewer kids means it's easier to save, but you'll have fewer possible caregivers in your later years. Larger families have more complex dynamics, but one of your adult children might step up to help you in old age.

How you'll balance child-rearing with income and savings is one of your first big challenges to address.

One Income or Two?

When you have children, money values can collide with your desire to spend time with your children. In 2024, the Bureau of Labor Statistics reported that both parents worked in about two-thirds of American families. What about your family? Should both parents work? It's a tricky decision that can touch deep emotional chords. And, of course, deciding to forgo one income for several years has major implications for your retirement savings and future lifestyle.

Here are a few questions to discuss with your partner:

- Do you both want one parent to be a full-time or part-time stay-at-home parent?

- If one of you earns substantially more, is the lower earner interested in taking on a full-time parenting role?

- If not, can you afford full-time childcare or perhaps work staggered hours or shifts to lessen the childcare costs?

- Can you keep retirement savings on track by cutting expenses?

Adding a child to your family calls for a whole new budget and savings plan. It may call for some sacrifices and attitude adjustments, which Chris illustrates with his friend's story.

———————— ☕ ————————

While Renee and her partner, Marcus, started their relationship with similar salaries, her social media marketing business took off, and her income skyrocketed. Eventually, she was making four times what he earned, which enabled the couple to enjoy a nice lifestyle.

When they decided to have a child, it didn't make financial sense for Renee to stay home. Marcus became a stay-at-home dad, but he wasn't thrilled about it.

One time, Marcus and I were at a bar with a group of friends. After he got a few drinks into him, he made a comment that worried me. When friends razzed him about being a stay-at-home dad, Marcus said, "What can I say? I've got a sugar mama!"

The next time I saw Marcus, I took him aside and replayed that comment. "Is that really how you think about Renee?" I asked. "Do you want her to quit her job and stay home while you work instead?"

"No, I love our lifestyle, and there's no way I could replace her income right now," he told me. "But there are times when I don't like how this situation makes me feel."

"Sounds like something you two should talk about," I suggested.

Fortunately, he did talk about his feelings with Renee, and he never made that comment again. Marcus and Renee both tell me their relationship has never been better. And now that their daughter is older and Marcus is working in a fulfilling job, both of their careers are soaring.

Happy parents work out their roles and learn to be content with them. And happy people often make more money. So, it's a win-win for your retirement savings.

Of course, money issues can be even more complicated if you're parenting solo.

Single with Kids

As a single parent, you're trying to be your kids' everything, including on the financial front. If you're divorced or separated and hoping child-support payments will see you through, think again. A study of female-headed households from 2020 to 2022 by the Annie E. Casie Foundation found less than one-quarter of these households received any amount of child support. If you're living in a casual situation with a partner, be aware that this arrangement could put you in a difficult monetary situation if it changes. Be prepared is all we're saying.

Need more income? Figure out how to go back to school or get additional training, even if it means relying on family help for a while. A lifetime of higher earnings will pay off for you and your children. It's worth the sacrifice of living beneath your means for a few years. A side hustle can also be a great way to move your financial status up the ladder.

Ways to Save in the Wonder Years

When that first baby comes along, many parents are living close to the bone. You may still be early in your career or stringing together multiple minimum-wage jobs to get by. Add baby costs, and you're cutting coupons for diapers and squeezing every penny until it hurts.

If you need childcare so you can go back to work, that's a growing, major cost, which the Department of Labor recently described as "untenable." Depending on how much care you need and where you live, that bill can resemble a second mortgage payment. If you have more than one child, this adds to the challenge.

Yet somehow, you have to put away money for retirement during these parenting years if you want to leverage the magic of compound interest to build wealth. It's a great time to reevaluate your spending and identify costs to cut.

Regularly meet with a financial advisor to learn if you're saving enough and investing your money aggressively enough to fund your retirement. You're still young and can take on more investment risk. If you make a bad bet, you have decades to earn more and make up lost ground. Start saving aggressively, ideally before the baby arrives, and keep up the momentum.

Here's another reason it's a critical time to save aggressively: By the time they toddle off to kindergarten, you'll be thinking about how to pay for your child's education in addition to saving for your retirement. What type of education will you save for?

Paying for Education: Hard Choices

Depending on where you live, your children's aptitudes, and the quality of your local public school system, you may be thinking about private school. A dozen years in private K–12 schools can easily cost more than four years at an elite college. (The website www.EducationData.org presents a wealth of data on the costs of private schools.) Perhaps your kids are bound for community college, where tuition costs are comparatively low or may be free for eligible students.

You'll have to decide where you stand on balancing your K–12 education, college, and retirement savings goals. Few families can afford to pay for private school and college while also building a substantial retirement account.

You could save for college and send your kids to public K–12 schools. Or you could prioritize private school and pay for college as it happens or get student loans or parent loans. Can you save for retirement and your children's education by sacrificing luxuries or taking a side job? Every parent's answer to these thorny questions will be different.

Some of us Boomer-generation parents were told by our parents to work our way through college and pay our own tuition costs—they either couldn't or wouldn't pay. Sadly, this approach is practically unworkable today due to soaring college costs. If you want your children to attend almost any four-year university, they'll probably need your financial help.

If you plan to delay retirement savings and pay for your children's education first, remember the story of Joe the accountant. Despite his professional salary, he ended up with little retirement savings when he waited until age fifty to start saving and investing.

One solution many parents don't explore is asking grandparents to help with education costs. Instead of watching them buy the grandkids toys they'll discard the day after their birthday party, ask them to help pay for college.

Grandparents can set up a flexible education savings account—or contribute to yours—and let you decide whether the money will go toward college or private school. One advantage of state college-savings plans: You don't have to figure out how to invest the savings for growth, and the appreciation is guaranteed. In our research, we found that you can also withdraw money from a Roth IRA for education without penalty. (Of course, tax laws are known to change, so always check with your accountant or the IRS website.)

In Chris's case, he chose to set up college funds for his grandkids, which enabled their parents to fund private schooling. They appreciated how that relieved financial stress on their education budgets.

If you haven't saved for college, the cost can be a shock. That's what happened to our friends, Andy and June. As you may recall, this couple married in midlife but continued to remain "financially single." They never planned their financial future for themselves as a couple or for their teenage son. Let's pick up their story.

As Andy and June neared retirement age, they realized they didn't have enough saved for retirement. They also didn't have a plan to cover college tuition and living expenses for their graduating high school senior who wanted to attend an expensive, out-of-state university.

"Our hearts were open," Marty told me of their romance. "We didn't think about money for all those years we were newlyweds and building a family together." Now, they are scrambling to make up for all the disadvantages created by their decision to remain financially single. And they face hard choices about whether to rob their retirement fund to pay for their son's college education and related expenses.

Currently, they are talking to their son about getting student loans and attending a more affordable in-state school to lessen their financial burden. We applaud their focus on keeping their retirement savings intact and not giving their son a free ride to an expensive, out-of-state college, which they truly cannot afford.

Another strategy can help pay for college—getting your kids to save some of the money they earn as they grow up and, especially, once they start working, so they can contribute to their college expenses.

Nine Ways to Get Kids to Save

One of the best gifts you can give your kids is the habit of saving money. Here are a few tips:

1. **Don't keep your savings habit a secret**—Talk with your children about how you're saving for vacations, a vehicle, and other financial goals and what you've decided to forgo to build your savings.
2. **Start small**—Give young children a small allowance with a certain portion earmarked for their piggy bank or savings account.
3. **Take field trips**—As they grow up, visit the bank to help kids understand where their money is and how it's growing.
4. **Inspire entrepreneurship**—Encourage older kids to try money-making projects, such as the classic lemonade stand or holding a garage sale.

5. **Give them a share**—Purchase a few shares of a dividend-paying stock for preteens and teens to get them interested in stock markets and investing.

6. **Gamify it**—Turn learning to save into a game with board and card games specifically designed to teach this important topic in a fun way. You can even use gamified savings apps, such as GoHenry, that reward your kids for deposits and encourage them to save more. The apps give you control over the account, while your kids participate and learn money skills.

7. **Holster your wallet**—When kids start whining for the latest expensive gadget, just say, "Well, let's see how much you've saved up!" Wait until they've saved their share for a purchase instead of whipping out the plastic.

8. **Offer work opportunities**—If your kids are truly dying for that item, you could help them save faster by identifying extra chores you could pay them to do. It might be a great way to clean your garage or tackle that gnarly weed patch!

9. **Consider a custodial Roth IRA**—When teens start to earn money, seed a Roth IRA you control until they reach the age of majority in your state. They can learn about investing and can even add some of their own income. Note that this strategy works best with trustworthy youths who won't cash out their accounts once they gain control.

Saving for a purchase helps kids learn how to postpone gratification, a trait that's in short supply in our TikTok age. Slowing down the shopping train saves you money, too.

Another big focus in this life stage is your family's health. Staying healthy will help you avoid medical debt, which can send even the best-laid retirement plan down a long and scary chute.

Earn a Healthy Savings Bonus

Now that you have children, your health habits aren't just about you. Your kids will learn good habits or poor ones from watching and emulating your behavior.

Start by maintaining continuous health insurance coverage for all family members, and make sure it includes mental health, too. All it takes is one year where you think, "Gee, the kids are doing great, they don't really need insurance" for a kiddo to break their leg, become suicidally depressed, or get diagnosed with a chronic illness. You know that would be the year it happens, right?

Protect your savings, and don't leave insurance gaps. If you have adopted or special needs kids, be sure to take advantage of any supplemental coverage they qualify for, such as Medicaid.

Next, create a family lifestyle that keeps everyone out of the doctor's office. Healthy habits start with the nutritional meals you plan and serve on a daily basis, with only the occasional pizza! Here are a few of our hard-won tips for eating healthily as a busy family:

- **Plan and prep ahead**—Set aside time each week to plan meals and prep ingredients. Chop veggies, marinate proteins, and batch cook grains or beans, so you can quickly throw meals together during the week.

- **Make healthy meals simple**—Focus on easy, nutritious meals that don't take much time to prepare. Think one-pan dishes, such as stir-fries and sheet-pan meals. Or try various slow-cooker recipes that you can start in the morning, and you can come home to a ready meal. Learn to make things like peanut butter or hummus from scratch.

- **Incorporate more plant-based foods**—Include more fruits, vegetables, and legumes in your meals. They're nutritious, affordable, and easy to add to nearly any dish, from salads to soups to pastas. Teach the difference between a complex and simple carbohydrate.

- **Get the whole family involved**—Engage your kids and partner in the kitchen! Whether it's chopping veggies, assembling tacos, or making smoothies, getting everyone involved helps lighten the load, teaches important skills, and makes healthy eating more fun.

By modeling healthy eating habits and serving nutritious meals, you'll help your kids avoid childhood obesity and juvenile diabetes, both of which are on the rise, according to the CDC. It's time to live your food values by establishing good eating habits to help your children develop a healthy relationship with food. This extra-helpful ladder in life will create a better, healthier lifestyle for you, your children, and possibly even your grandchildren!

Unfortunately, many kids today don't just subsist on junk—they rarely leave the couch and can't do a single push-up. It's time to get your family moving. Ideally, together.

Get Up and Boogie

Find exercises everyone can participate in together, even if it's just functional fitness tweaks, such as parking farther from the department store, biking out to dinner, or installing a chin-up bar in a doorway. Do an online search on the phrase *functional fitness tips*, and you'll discover lots of creative ways to work exercises into your daily activities.

Think of keeping your family healthy as another kind of investment. Fewer doctor visits mean more money for retirement, given the co-pays and deductibles most health plans require. Your "let's stay healthy together" strategy will help you bypass some expensive healthcare chutes that can set back your retirement plan by years or even decades.

Get creative about activities your crew would enjoy. When Tracy was raising two step-children who often had as many as nine visiting cousins, her home's backyard volleyball court was a center of activity, along with many other activities, including skiing and playing softball games. In bad weather, she cracked out the Nintendo Wii and Guitar Hero games for indoor fun that encouraged movement.

Be Resolute with Your Retirement Savings

You may have noticed, with some parents, avoiding conflict with their kids has transitioned into ceding power to them. When this happens, kids can get the latest electronic gadgets they want or the sports car they "have to have," and the parents' retirement plan can suffer. Chris recently chatted with a friend who was trapped in this alarming cycle.

Jim was nearing retirement age, and I asked him if he had saved enough money. He said no, adding that he and his wife Judy were struggling to catch up. They both have careers but earn moderate incomes for their upscale area of Massachusetts.

Then I asked where their son, Adam, a high school senior, was going to attend college. They named a state university in another state.

"Why that school?" I asked him. "If he's going to a state school, why not send him to your state's school? You'd probably pay two-thirds less with in-state tuition."

"Oh, this is the school he wants to attend," Jim replied.

"Do you have enough saved in a college account to pay for this out-of-state college?" I asked.

"No," he replied. "We're taking the tuition payments out of our retirement savings."

This couple needs to give their son a hard no to attending a college they simply cannot afford when an equivalent Massachusetts college can fulfill his academic needs and better fit their budget. But over the years, they handed over more and more control until they simply gave their son whatever he wanted—even if it could leave them struggling financially. Some of this behavior is driven by the fact that they want their only child to have all the finer things they didn't have growing up.

After a chat with us about their retirement prospects, Jim and Judy began to explore student loans to pay for their son's chosen school instead of emptying their retirement account.

We know this isn't a parenting book, but it's an important topic to touch on. Establishing a healthy parent-child relationship can save your retirement when your college-age kids need money or your grown kids ask for financial support.

Meanwhile, you've got kids at home, and your days are packed with activities. It's rewarding yet grueling, and the years fly by. For now, kids are your world. It's easy to look up eighteen or twenty years later and realize you never started a college savings account or put a dime away for retirement.

Even though this is one of the hardest stages of life when it comes to saving money for your retirement, we implore you to do your best to make it happen. Keep saving, review your retirement savings account frequently, and regularly meet with your financial advisor to ensure your investments are on track.

Top Seven Takeaways for Parents

Here are key points to keep your retirement plan on track while you raise children:

1. **Create a budget**—Ideally, you should do this before your first child arrives.

2. **Focus on earning enough to save for retirement**—Decide if you'll both work while the kids

are young. Do everything possible to earn more and save more during your parenting years, even if it involves some sacrifices.

3. **Teach your kids to plan and save**—You can do this by modeling good planning and saving skills yourself.

4. **Save for kids' education**—As you do, decide how to balance education costs with your retirement savings.

5. **Eat healthily and exercise together**—It's great for family bonding, will improve everyone's health, and is a money saver.

6. **Establish a healthy parent-child relationship**— Set appropriate boundaries from the get-go. It'll be easier to say no later when your grown kids want financial help.

7. **Assess your progress on retirement savings**— Seek help from a financial advisor to ensure your investments are on track.

Sticking with these principles will help you prepare for the next stage of life, which can be even more complicated.

Navigating Midlife Challenges
While Staying on Course

J∪ST WHEN YOU THINK you have life figured out you may find yourself entering one of the most transformative stages yet. As they reach middle age, many people hope to thrive both personally and professionally. If you're fortunate, that's exactly what's happening with you.

You may have created a solid career plan, and after two or three decades in your field, your career now offers both financial growth and personal satisfaction. Your children are leaving the nest, likely heading off to college or starting on their own career paths. You've also been diligent about saving and investing for retirement.

If this describes your life, that's fantastic. However, many middle-aged individuals face a different reality.

During your forties and fifties, you can find yourself in a challenging situation, often referred to as the *sandwich years*, because you're in the middle of two sets of tough responsibilities. On one hand, you may be caring for aging parents who haven't adequately prepared for their own retirement. If they are divorced, widowed, or disabled, they may need help with daily tasks, healthcare support, and even financial support.

At the same time, you could be supporting your young adult child. Perhaps your son or daughter moves back home after college or has work-related issues, such as a layoff or not earning enough to support themself, or returns to the nest while recovering from a relationship breakup.

These sandwich-generation responsibilities can put your finances on shaky ground. Will you keep building wealth for retirement or face major financial setbacks that send you hurtling down a chute?

These midlife years hold complex financial and emotional challenges. How can you sail through the sandwich years with peace of mind, helping family while keeping your own retirement plan on track? It begins with taking a fresh look at your values.

Your value system may have served you well as you grew your family and career. But now you face additional burdens that could tax your relationship with your spouse or partner to the utmost—issues you two may never have discussed before.

You may have imagined that your parents have saved for their secure retirement, are staying healthy, and will stay together. You may have expected your children to go off to great colleges and straight into well-paid careers and independent lives. But that rosy picture doesn't square with today's reality for many families.

In 2024, skyrocketing housing prices, high student-loan debt, and an uncertain job market resulted in more than half of young adults living with their parents, as reported in a June 2024 *USA Today* article.

At the same time, the National Council on Aging reported the startling fact that many of our elders live in poverty, trying to get by on Social Security alone. For many, those monthly benefits are meager. According to the Center on Budget and Policy Priorities, the average monthly payout is less than $1,900 a month. And that's *before* Medicare premiums and taxes are deducted.

Consider, too, that when half of all marriages end in divorce it translates into more aging parents living alone. That means more pressure on their adult children to offer financial assistance.

To sum up, the odds that your family's older or younger generation—or both—might need help from you are pretty good. It's time to revisit your core values and contemplate how they can guide you through these twin challenges.

If you're in a marriage or other long-term partnership, take the time to discuss how your values call you to respond to the potential issues of your parents and young adult children *before* a need arises. Later, it'll be easier to have thoughtful, clear-headed conversations about what you feel comfortable doing and can afford in terms of assistance.

If you wait until a crisis occurs, you might make snap decisions that you might regret later. Here's a real-life example of a long-married couple we know whose adult child ran into money trouble.

———————— ☕ ————————

During a weeknight dinner, Claire and Lester received an unexpected call from their son, Ethan, who revealed he had been laid off, was broke, and was facing eviction. Concerned for his well-being, they swiftly drove ninety minutes to move him back into his childhood home.

Months later, they realized they had a growing problem. Ethan was only working sporadically and showed little motivation to find full-time employment. Instead, he took long showers, languished in front of the TV, consumed all their food, and contributed nothing to the household.

Claire wanted to establish rules and set a timeline for his stay, but Lester enjoyed having Ethan home and hesitated to impose limits. They recognized that their well-meaning offer had turned into a situation that undermined Ethan's independence, leaving him feeling humiliated and depressed rather than encouraged to get back on his feet.

At the same time, the stress on this couple's relationship was incredible—until the day their son got an offer to share a house with a friend and suddenly moved out again, with no savings to back him up. They're braced for the pattern to repeat itself but ready to set boundaries next time.

To foster a positive family dynamic, plan ahead and discuss boundaries and expectations when your adult children move out. Determine how you can support them, whether through financial help or allowing them to return home temporarily, and take steps to create a comfortable balance for everyone. When challenges arise, clearly communicate your willingness, level of support, and duration of support, which will help to ensure a smooth experience. Early conversations can build a strong foundation and clarify everyone's needs and expectations.

Also, consider your parents' needs and engage in open discussions with them to strengthen family bonds and create a solid plan that honors everyone's requirements.

How to Talk with Your Parents About Their Money

Here's a hard truth of life: We can't make our parents do anything. We wish the best for them, but they're living their own lives. They may take good care of their health or smoke like chimneys and eat KFC every day. And they may be diligent retirement savers or never put away a dime.

If it's the latter, at some point they may need financial assistance. And now's the time to find out. Americans are living longer, and care for aging parents can be a long-term commitment.

Sizing up your parents' current financial situation helps you understand the support they may need in the future. Just as you did with your grown kids, this chat will help you clarify your values, expectations, and boundaries. If you have siblings, this conversation should include them as well as your partner.

You're probably aware of your parents' lifestyle and general spending habits, but money is a taboo subject in many families. And looks can be deceiving. Your parents may appear to have a well-funded, secure lifestyle, but they could be steadily emptying their retirement accounts to support it.

Let your parents know you want to have an important talk with them, and choose a time when you can all focus without distractions. Tell them you'd like to know more about their financial situation in case you can offer help or advice. Hopefully, they'll agree to discuss this topic openly with you. If so, here are some questions to ask:

- Can we learn where all your important papers are, computer passwords to access various accounts and digital documents, and information about your financial accounts?

- What are your expenses? Could they be lowered?

- Do you have a mortgage? If so, what would it take to pay it off?

- What is your monthly income from all sources (work, Social Security, pensions, retirement accounts, residuals, other sources)?

- What are your assets? For instance, do you own your home outright, or have you built up equity?

- Are you depleting your savings and, if so, at what rate?

- Do you worry about running out of money?

- Do you have long-term care insurance? If so, what does it cover?

- Have you done any estate planning? Do you have a will, an advance directive for medical care, and a durable power of attorney?

- If you have a will, who is the executor and what is their contact information?

- Have you set up a trust for heirs and, if so, what's in it? How is it structured? If needed, could you withdraw money from that trust to support yourselves?

- If you have money put aside for family members as an inheritance, would you consider transferring some or all of it to us early, so we can use it to help you?

Yes, we can feel you cringe at the idea of asking your parents some of these sensitive financial questions. But without this conversation, you may get hit by a tsunami wave of money trouble one day. It's better to be forewarned about what's coming and have time to help your parents adjust their course, if necessary.

This advice goes double if you're contemplating inviting a parent (or both parents) into your home. You really need them to be fully honest and open about multiple nuts-and-bolts matters, including their financial standing, health issues, and legal papers, such as wills and trusts, as well as their hopes and fears about their retirement and elder years. Perhaps you can say, "We're happy to have you, and we want to lead with our hearts. But we need to know what we're getting into."

If you're in the dark about your parents' finances and hesitate to have "the talk," here's a story about a business executive we'll call Tom and his free-spending parents, which may help you build up your courage.

———— ☕ ————

Around the time he hit forty, Tom found out his parents were financially unprepared for retirement. It was a shock because Steve and Sylvia appeared to be doing great. They'd recently taken out a fifteen-year mortgage for a large, new home in an upscale town in Wisconsin with a three-car garage for their flashy new cars.

Then they came clean to him. After making all those big purchases, they were now broke! Their monthly expenses included a $4,500 mortgage payment and $2,300 in car payments. Despite their empty bank accounts, the overspending continued. Sylvia had plans to host a lavish baby shower for one of Tom's sisters.

Tom had to have a tough talk with his parents. They agreed to sell their big home within the year, sell the third car, and ask someone else to host that over-the-top baby shower. Tom is helping them with some bills through this transition while guiding them to become self-sufficient once they reduce their expenses.

If you thought asking your parents about their retirement savings would be awkward, imagine how difficult it was for Tom to have that conversation with his free-spending parents. Fortunately, Tom has a clear sense of his boundaries. He will not fund their lavish lifestyle. He is willing to help them temporarily while they transition to a lifestyle they can afford, but they must tighten their belts and learn to live within their means.

You can face tough questions during the sandwich phase. Are you willing to give your parents money to live on, even if it wipes out your own retirement savings? Are you willing to continue supporting your young adult children, even if your savings plan suffers?

Agree on what you're willing to do for adult children and parents in need in terms of financial and emotional support. Think twice before you put your retirement savings at risk. It could set you up to repeat the same mistakes your parents made, ending up retired without adequate resources.

Love on the Rocks

As you hit midlife, your relationship with your partner can show the strain. You've been busy raising kids, socializing with friends, and building careers with scant time together as a couple. You've grown and changed, and your lifestyle has evolved. Has all this brought you closer together or created a rift?

Ask yourself if you feel your relationship is still healthy or if you have concerns. Is your partner helping you be your best self and supporting your caregiving efforts?

If you feel you've grown apart, have issues in your relationship, or your values are no longer aligned, pay attention. Because if you aren't happy together as a twosome, you may not survive the squeeze of the sandwich years.

If you have issues to hash out, sit down and talk, find a therapist or faith-based counselor who can help you reconnect and strengthen your bond. It's worth it because divorce is such a disastrous emotional and financial chute. Communicate openly and honestly with your partner. Be guided by your values as you take care of yourself and others in your life.

Important Decisions in the Sandwich Years

Once you've talked with each other, your grown kids, and your parents, you can create a game plan for your sandwich phase. Be honest with yourself about your own income prospects for the coming years, your mental resilience for these added stressors, and your interest or ability to provide hands-on caregiving.

Figure out your financial bandwidth for helping relatives and stick to it. Otherwise, the sandwich years can knock you off the ladder you've been climbing to your dream retirement. Here are some questions to discuss with your partner or to ask yourself if you're single:

- How much disposable income do we have that we both feel comfortable using to help parents and adult children?

- Can we cut some expenses to free up more resources?

- Can we ask parents to downsize their house or cut their expenses to reduce our cost burden?

- Would we borrow money to help parents if we don't have enough? If so, how much?

- Would we consider borrowing from our retirement fund to help family?

- Do we both plan to continue working, either in full-time or part-time jobs?

- How much is our estimated annual income for the next five years?

- Can we afford to hire caregiving help for parents if we cannot fulfill that role?

If your "retirement plan" is to work forever and never retire, thinking you don't need to save, please reconsider. Understand that it's rarely possible or even desirable to work into your seventies, eighties, or nineties.

Foresee a day when you can't work or won't work anymore, and you'll need a retirement fund to support you. Prioritize safeguarding your retirement savings as you strive to meet family members' needs.

Most of us can't control when our parents start saving for retirement, how much they save, or how they invest those savings. When it comes to your children, though, you can (and should) educate them about money—and the importance of having savings—so they can always land on their feet.

How to Keep Grown Kids Independent

No matter how well you have planned and saved, if you haven't taught your children how to be financially self-reliant and set clear boundaries about supporting them as adults, trouble may be lurking on the horizon. This story from a friend illustrates what we mean.

———————— ☕ ————————

Art and Sherry both worked while raising their two children. They expected to enjoy a nice retirement with the combination of his union pension and the $250,000 retirement account they'd built through the decades. After all, they already lived in the Deep South, an area where many people retire thanks to the low cost of living.

Their golden years were on track, and Art had already retired when their grown daughter Sue—who always swore she'd never marry or have kids—fell for the wrong guy, got pregnant, and needed their help. In an instant, their retirement plan disintegrated.

The father of Sue's child quickly vanished. Overnight, she became the sole parent of a new baby in the midst of the COVID-19 pandemic. She lost her waitressing job and was struggling to pay bills. Art and Sherry were stunned to learn that Sue had saved nothing in over a decade of working.

The couple found themselves paying for numerous cross-country trips to visit Sue in the Northeast to help her and to spend time with their new grandson. They also began paying many of Sue's bills. After all, they didn't want to see their daughter and grandson out on the street.

Soon, they were tapping into their 401(k) savings. After a few years of this costly back-and-forth routine, they moved Sue and her now-toddler son into their home to save money. They weren't crazy about giving up their privacy, but they needed to take them in because their retirement account was empty, and they could no longer afford to support the two households.

Now, they pay all of Sue's family expenses, and at nearly seventy, Art has taken a minimum-wage retail job to help rebuild their retirement fund. This unexpected family event led to a devastating chute for Art and Sherry's retirement plan and financial security.

If you have adult children, do you talk with them about the importance of saving and investing or living by their values and choosing a mate wisely? If not, we recommend you start having these conversations with your grown kids now. Don't wait for things to fall apart.

Chris finds that his adult children will happily discuss their values with him. But when it comes to whether they're saving for retirement or even whether they've built an emergency fund, they clam up. If you want to discuss uncomfortable money topics, one approach is to talk about your own situation. Explain what you are doing to save. Share how you've invested your money. From there, it's an easier pivot to inquire what they're doing along these lines.

While you're having this money talk, share your limits regarding supporting adult children. You may have the resources to assist them in an emergency—or not. In addition, address your feelings around what you think your role should be when grown kids struggle. You may want to help them out, or you may think they'll acquire better life skills if they solve their own problems. You may be wary that helping them with money once could lead to repeated requests for a bailout.

Start front-loading expectations around your help and boundaries while your kids are young. It's a low-stress conversation when you're handing out allowances or casually sharing money management tips compared with the one that happens when they turn up on your doorstep, broke and asking for help.

If your kids fail to build a solid career and emergency savings account or your parents come to you in financial trouble, you may need to make one of life's toughest calls—whether to take them into your home.

Would You Take In Your Parents or Adult Children?

If your parents or grown children can't afford their own housing, you'll find yourself at a crossroads that will require careful consideration. Once you take family members into your home, it's not always easy to move them back out again.

Yes, it's a financial decision, but it's also a decision that touches on deeply held beliefs you may have about the nature of family. In some cultures, parents commonly live with their adult children and grandchildren. In other cultures, having elderly parents living in your home means a loss of privacy, which may not work for you.

Ten Questions for Families to Ask Before Taking In a Relative

If you're contemplating taking in a parent or grown child, here are some discussion questions to help you gain clarity:

1. Do we both feel that having a family member (or multiple family members) move in with us is the right thing to do?

2. Do we physically have space in our home to do this? Will we need to make alterations to our home, such as building a wheelchair ramp or adding a bedroom? If so, can we cover those costs?

3. Are we clear about our financial standing to understand how this could affect us now and in the future? Are we willing to accept these new costs?

4. Can we consult with a financial planner to learn how this decision would affect our retirement plan?

5. Have these family members been transparent about their finances so that we understand the full scope of the help they need, both now and in the future?

6. If they have an income, whether from a job, pension, savings, or Social Security, can they contribute to daily bills and necessities, such as rent or mortgage? If so, how much can they contribute,

and how much do we think is appropriate? Are these contributions essential to ensure we avoid debt, continue building our retirement account, or (in the case of adult children) reinforce responsible money management?

7. Can our siblings help pay some of the costs of housing to help our parents?

8. Do these family members have healthcare coverage and, if so, what kind? Will they need any major medical help soon? If so, who will pay the co-pays, deductibles, and other out-of-pocket costs?

9. Do we have a list of boundaries, house rules, and expectations for the family members joining our household? (If not, take the time to create and discuss this list well before the moving date.)

10. If this is a temporary move, have we decided on a time frame for this stay that everyone agrees to follow? Have we established agreed-upon consequences if they do not meet that time frame?

Clarify and agree on your boundaries before you pull up to mom's place with a moving van. If you do take in a relative, revisit the house rules on a regular basis to see if they're still working or need to be adjusted.

If you or your partner don't feel comfortable taking in a relative, it probably shouldn't happen. For instance, listen to this couple's conversation about taking in a parent.

――――――― ☕ ―――――――

Martin was nearing his sixties when his widowed mother started needing assistance. Betty had a long history of mental-health problems and had become increasingly confused and paranoid.

He brought up the idea to his wife, Julie, of moving his mom in with them and their three school-age children.

"Mom has Social Security and her savings, and she could pay her own way here," he said. "It could help with our budget, and she'd save a lot of money instead of going into assisted living, which she doesn't want to do anyway."

Betty had always been unkind to Julie and often criticized their children, so the idea of bringing her into their home was a definite no for Julie.

"How do you imagine this would work out?" she asked Martin. "Betty is eighty-one, and her mom lived to be nearly one hundred. This could be a long journey, and it would be challenging to ask her to leave once she gets comfortable here, relying on us for support. Plus, she's not even civil to you sometimes, and you're her favorite child! She's always had issues with me. You know her pattern. She embraces every new place for a short while and then begins to complain about everything.

"I want to protect our children from her instability," she continued. "We've put so much effort into creating a peaceful home and instilling positive traits like kindness and good manners in our kids. I think that would all change with her here."

After considering Julie's comments, Martin researched assisted living options near their home. He toured a highly rated place within his mom's budget and found it to be clean, well run, and professionally staffed. Betty reluctantly moved *in but soon adapted and made friends there. Martin was able to visit frequently and run errands for her now that she lived closer.*

Since Betty lived in her own place, Martin could bring their kids to visit on Betty's good days. That gave grandma a chance to see the grandkids, and it gave Martin and Julie peace of mind, knowing they could quickly end the visit if Betty became verbally abusive. Betty's move to an assisted living apartment was the best solution for the entire family and well worth the added expense.

Not every family can withstand the strain of taking in a relative, so be realistic and know your limits. If you mutually decide to take in a relative, consider a weekly family meeting as a forum to discuss any issues that crop up.

Financially, don't be shy about asking everyone to pitch in who possibly can. If you're doing the heavy lifting of housing financially strapped parents, then your siblings should help defray your costs, especially if it stretches your budget, and they can afford it. You shouldn't be tumbling down a chute to a poverty-stricken retirement while siblings sacrifice nothing.

Beyond the costs, you'll devote precious time and energy assisting parents and adult children who live with you. As you progress through the sandwich years, it's more important than ever to focus on preserving your health, so you will have the energy, patience, and peace of mind to successfully juggle all your responsibilities.

Healthy Strategies to Keep Going Strong

Midlife is often when health challenges begin in earnest as stress from multiple responsibilities can multiply. Busy days can mean skipping workouts, sacrificing good eating habits, and gaining weight year after year. (The National Library of Medicine reports that "ten-year weight gain is a serious problem within the US adult population.") Symptoms for various conditions, such as diabetes or heart disease, may begin to appear if you're not treating your body right.

Hopefully, you've built relationships with key health-care providers, so they know your history and can spot any troubling new symptoms. Don't miss regular checkups, and be sure to take your doctor's advice to heart.

Let us put it plainly: Healthy eating and regular exercise are must-dos for sandwich-generation adults. You can't keep taking care of everyone else if you're frequently sick or simply too exhausted to function.

Nourish your body with food that energizes you because caring for others starts with caring for yourself. Juggling work and household responsibilities along with kids' extracurricular activities and your parents' frequent doctor appointments takes stamina fueled by nourishing foods—not a diet of drive-through burgers and highly processed frozen meals loaded with salt and saturated fat.

As you move through midlife, you've entered the "use it or lose it" years. If you'd rather age like a mountain goat than a three-toed sloth, make strength training and cardio activities part of your weekly rhythm. Your future self will thank you every time you carry in the groceries without a second thought.

Even when fitness is a priority, caregiving brings its own mental and emotional challenges. Protect your energy with regular self-care, so you can continue to show up for others without running on empty.

Fundamentals of Sustainable Caregiving

If you're contemplating taking a parent into your home who might live for years, you'll need a lot of stamina. As we noted previously, the caregiving burden falls disproportionately on women. About two-thirds of family caregivers are female, according to the US Bureau of Labor Statistics. Know that caregiver burnout is real and all too common. A 2025 study by the Family Caregiver Alliance found that up to 70 percent of family caregivers are clinically depressed.

How can you stay positive and mentally strong as you cope with additional family responsibilities? Start by staying in touch with your feelings around the burdens you carry. How are you doing, really? You may put on a smiling face for the people you care for, but behind the facade you may struggle.

If you're feeling alone as a caregiver, know that support groups are virtually everywhere. Start with your own healthcare plan and see if they offer caregiver support groups. If not, a quick online search for caregiver support in your city should turn up multiple resources.

It's tremendously comforting and uplifting to meet others who are tackling similar challenges. You may get good ideas to handle problems you're having and even make a new friend or two. It'll do wonders for your mental health.

It Takes a Village

Speaking of support, you shouldn't be a family caregiver alone. Who is your backup? Reach out to family, friends, or your faith network and let them know you've taken on new responsibilities. Here are a few ways to lighten your load and make your caregiving duties less stressful and more sustainable:

- Find babysitters for younger kids who can also drive the kids to their extracurricular activities.

- Use a driver service to take parents to hair appointments, the local senior center, and gatherings with their friends.

- Explore whether a paid caregiver could sub for you sometimes. Even just two hours a day could make a big difference.

- Sign up for a meal train with friends or your faith community, so you can cook fewer meals. Research home-delivered meal programs in your area, such as Meals on Wheels.

- Recruit a friend who's willing to listen to you vent and will help you brainstorm workable solutions to your challenges.

Finances may be one of the many worries on your mind as a family caregiver. If so, relieve that stress by reviewing your income-generating, saving, and investing plans. Make sure caregiving doesn't break the bank.

Your Midlife Money Checkup

You may be busier than ever, but don't ignore your savings during the sandwich years. Too many people sign up for automatic deposits into their 401(k), choose a few mutual funds in that account, and then never check to see how their account is doing. For thirty years.

We've talked about using company 401(k) plans to build retirement wealth, but according to a 2024 AARP report, 57 million Americans don't have access to one. And many people struggle to save on their own. Whether you save for retirement through a company 401(k) or on your own, don't just throw money in a pot for your whole career and ignore it. You've reached an age in which growing your money really matters. The number of years you have left to earn, save, and invest is limited.

You may have multiple 401(k)s and IRAs due to job changes. List all your accounts, find your statements, and look at the big picture of your current savings. Learn how you're invested now, so you can see your progress and how that might project into the future.

Have you been holding all your savings in a money market account or certificates of deposit (CDs) because you're averse to risk and leery of the stock market? If so, it's time to get that money into long-term investments that produce better returns. The interest you earn on a savings account won't keep up with inflation, much less meaningfully grow your money.

This may be the time for you to adopt a less risk-averse investing approach to get higher returns. When we say this, we don't mean start buying Bitcoin. Only invest money you can afford to lose in unproven vehicles, such as cryptocurrency. These types of investments may yield sky-high returns today but could be worthless tomorrow.

Are your accounts still too skinny? You can either cut expenses or increase income to accelerate your savings rate (or both). One ripe area for cuts is reducing debt. Review the interest rates you're paying for your mortgage, car loan, and credit card balances. Pay off the highest-interest debt first to reduce your total interest payments. Consider whether you can consolidate or refinance any loans at a lower interest rate.

If you are serious about building retirement wealth, you should meet with a certified financial advisor by midlife. Be sure it's someone you're comfortable with. Here is a checklist of possible questions to ask at that meeting:

- If I keep saving at current rates, will I have enough put away by my retirement age for a secure retirement?

- Am I on track to have enough to pay for my children's college education?

- If the answer to both questions is no, how should I balance these two saving goals?

- What is my current asset allocation mix between riskier (stock funds) and less risky (bond funds) investments?

- What do my current investments yield in terms of dividends or distributions that I can reinvest or spend?

- Do you think I should adjust my mix because various accounts have become overweighted one way or the other? Or because I'm older now?

- I'm considering diversifying further and taking on more risk. What other asset classes or vehicles would you recommend?

An investment management pro can help you decide on a mix of investments that suit your goals. Your advisor can also help you understand all the investments you select, so you can continue to become more financially astute.

If you're not paying attention to your investments, you may be taking on more risk than you realize, or you may be invested too conservatively. This is because investments gain or lose value over time and that changes how much you have invested in each mutual fund, exchange-traded fund (ETF), or other security.

Also, most portfolios are set up to DRIP—this stands for *dividend reinvestment plan*. What does this mean? If any of your mutual funds pay distributions or dividends, that money is reinvested back into that same fund and is not used to further diversify your holdings. You may have started out with 60 percent in stock-holding mutual funds and 40 percent in bonds, but over time the DRIPs can throw that percentage out of whack.

It's time to review and rebalance your portfolio to ensure it has the right risk ratio. You may choose to take on more risk now if you need to catch up or perhaps move some money into less risky vehicles because you're getting closer to retirement.

It also could be time to further diversify your investments into asset types beyond stocks and bonds. Be sure to talk with your financial advisor if you're thinking about buying, say, real estate or individual stocks. Ditto for buying real estate investment trusts (REITs), high-yield ("junk") bonds, precious metals, futures, or options. These higher-risk vehicles could boost your returns, but a novice shouldn't plunge into these without understanding their risks and how they work.

Finding a Pro

Financially speaking, your relationship with your investment pro may be one of the most rewarding professional relationships in your life. Of course, it's critically important to find a certified representative who always has your best interests at heart and is absolutely trustworthy. This person's guidance can be an essential ladder to your secure retirement.

Here's a story about looking for trustworthy advice. One evening, we were invited to an investment seminar held at a nearby college and run by a money management firm in Florida. Putting on our amateur social scientist hats, we went because we were curious to hear their spiel and get a sense of the other attendees' levels of retirement preparedness.

The two presenters were in cheap suits—a pair of middle-aged guys going through the motions of a presentation they'd clearly done dozens of times before. They started by asking the audience of about forty attendees if they knew what their IRAs were currently invested in. Only a few people raised their hands.

From there, they moved into a slideshow that was clearly designed to scare the heck out of us. You know the type of presentation: "The world is on fire—inflation and higher future taxes are going to leave you in poverty unless you migrate to a Roth to save on taxes, and you need us to manage it." That was roughly the drift. The goal was to get us all to sign up to have them migrate our traditional IRA funds to a Roth IRA to save on taxes in retirement.

It was a high-pressure sales pitch and didn't provide any details on how they would invest our money or what they would do differently from other money management firms. It was just, "Give us your money, and you can go back to not thinking about how you're invested."

We were very turned off and, needless to say, didn't sign up. But we felt heavy at the thought that the attendees who hopped on this Roth train may be getting taken advantage of without having the right people taking care of them and their retirement money.

The presenters also did something that's become a pet peeve of ours while researching this book. They showed us how their investment plan would make your money last until you're seventy-five years old. They did not show an alternative projection for how long your money could last if you lived to age ninety, which more of us are doing, as noted in a 2024 Pew Research Center report. That felt irresponsible.

While you're looking for a trustworthy financial advisor, know that some of these professionals also advise on insurance products. This is another key area to look at when it comes to saving for retirement.

Is Your Income Safe?

You've reached a stage in life where, hopefully, your hard work is paying off, and you're earning well. Your loved ones rely on that stability, which makes this the perfect time to think about life insurance. It may not be the most exciting topic, but it's one of the most powerful ways to protect your family's future and ensure the life you're building for them stays secure, no matter what.

If the loss of your income would be a disaster, term life insurance can provide a payout that gives your family breathing room to make alternative plans. It's called *term* because it's for a finite period. If you have fifteen years left before retirement, you'd likely choose a fifteen-year term. Costs depend on the payout amount and term length you choose. The big downside is that if you don't die during the term, your premiums are gone, and your heirs receive nothing.

Want an insurance policy that's also an investment, with coverage that continues throughout your life? Then look for whole life insurance. You guessed it; this policy is in effect until you die.

BIG TIP: You can set up whole life insurance in a way to ensure it will build cash value over time, and you can sometimes borrow from it as well, at favorable terms. So, this pool of premium cash can serve as an emergency fund. If you lack other assets, whole life insurance also gives you a way to leave something to heirs.

An advantage of whole life policies is that many come with a guaranteed return rate. Your money grows over time, and you don't have to figure out how to make it happen. If you hate managing your investments, this can be a nice option.

An advantage of both insurance types is that insurance payouts are generally tax-free for your heirs.

Life insurance products have grown increasingly complex, so be sure to locate a trusted, fee-only advisor to help you choose the most appropriate policy for your situation. Read any policy carefully, and make sure you understand how it works.

Long-Term Care Insurance: Age Matters

Let's look at another important type of life insurance, which is really more of a quality-of-life insurance. We're referring to long-term care (LTC) insurance. We know—you're thinking you may never need nursing-home care due to age or disability and, in any case, that scenario is far off in the future.

Then why buy LTC insurance now? Because you can afford LTC insurance now. If you wait until you're sixty or sixty-five, you'll get an unpleasant surprise. The premiums for these policies skyrocket as you age. Hop online and run some numbers on a long-term care insurance website to see the cost difference for a forty-five-year-old versus a sixty-five-year-old.

When he was sixty-five, Chris investigated getting LTC insurance for himself, and the premium costs were shocking. He passed.

If you delay purchasing LTC insurance, you may find it's too late to get an affordable rate. Without it, if you need care, your options are grim.

State-funded nursing homes are depressing, sometimes even dangerous places to live. We know from sad experience because we checked out some of these facilities for a relative. The Medicare website (www.Medicare.gov) is a great resource to help you understand what LTC insurance will cover as well as how to find providers and evaluate facilities.

For a real-life example of how this can matter, we'll share a brief story of an elderly relative who developed Alzheimer's disease in recent years. Her family is heartbroken about her dementia and how it is affecting her cognitive abilities and their relationships. Making matters worse, they didn't plan for such a possibility. Now, they're paying large sums of money every month for this unexpected, ongoing care. You can bet it's taking a major bite out of their monthly budget.

If they'd taken the time to learn about assisted living and memory care costs, which can easily reach $10,000 a month for a quality facility, they could have purchased an LTC policy or started a savings fund against such a possible future cost. Now, they have the pain of helping a loved one who may not even recognize family members anymore while also coping with major financial stress.

Are You Covered?

Beyond life insurance, take a look at the coverages you carry for home and auto insurance. If you've acquired expensive "toys" over time, perhaps a boat or RV, make sure your home insurance has enough coverage for the contents of your house and garage. If your home has increased in value, make sure coverage would truly enable you to rebuild at current new-home construction prices. And make sure your car insurance goes beyond the minimum requirements, or you can get hit with a large medical bill if you cause an accident and injure someone.

Finally, if you own a business, make sure you have business insurance. A business owner's policy provides a layer of protection between your personal assets and anyone who might sue the business, and it can help protect you from business losses or liabilities.

In Case of Emergency . . .

As you get older and life gets more complicated, the need grows for an emergency fund with enough to cover three to six months of expenses. Build your emergency fund in a high-yield savings or money market account with cash you could access quickly. You'll be glad you have it if you or your spouse gets laid off or someone in your family has a medical crisis. As the saying goes, expect the unexpected. This story about Diana and Norm's unexpected medical situation illustrates why everyone needs an emergency fund.

————— ☕ —————

Our friends recently faced a crisis when their teenage child required a month of inpatient care to receive proper treatment. When the hospital's billing administrator reviewed the costs with them, Diana and Norm were relieved to learn that insurance would cover most of the expenses, but they'd still be responsible for a $2,700 out-of-pocket bill.

"No problem," Diana replied calmly. Their emergency fund could easily handle it. Her only question: "How would you prefer we transfer the payment?"

The billing supervisor blinked in surprise. "Wait, you have the money?" he asked, clearly thrown off. He had assumed he would walk them through a payment plan. "We almost never hear that," he added. "Hardly anyone has a few thousand dollars ready for something like this."

When a crisis hits, it's a relief to know you can deal with it without money worries. Think about how you can create or build up your emergency fund. Perhaps a tax refund, performance bonus, or other unexpected chunk of money can go straight into the emergency fund. If it's an unusual or one-time source of income, you'll never miss it, and you'll sleep better at night knowing it's there if you need it.

You've Got This

The sandwich years can make you feel like the bills will never stop. But, at some point, your sandwich-generation time will end. Parents move to assisted living or pass on, and your grown children land great jobs, and off they go. As the decks clear, it's time to take a breath and turn your focus back to your own life.

You've been saving for retirement, but now it's time to begin planning your retirement. It's starting to come into view over the horizon. And you may have learned some lessons when caring for parents or other elderly relatives that may have changed your attitude about the kind of retirement you want—lessons that will help you visualize the healthy, wealthy retirement you want to enjoy.

Top Ten Takeaways for the Sandwich Years

The complexities of having parents or adult children who need assistance mean it's time to revisit many of the fundamental principles you've used as your guide throughout your life. Keep these top ten takeaways in mind:

1. **Review your values**—Ensure you and your partner have a clear and shared list of values as they apply to helping parents and adult children.

2. **Renew your relationship with your partner**—Keep it strong, or it may snap under the sandwich-years strain.

3. **Talk with your parents about their money**—Know what you're dealing with now to prepare for future possibilities.

4. **Know your caretaking limits**—Do an honest assessment of your financial, physical, and emotional capabilities and limits.

5. **Keep grown kids independent**—Teach them to save and be financially self-reliant.

6. **Make caretaking decisions together**—This is an especially important point when taking a family member into your home.

7. **Don't neglect your health**—You're older and caring for others now. Eat nutritious meals, exercise, and take time for yourself.

8. **Prioritize mental and physical self-care**—This will help to ensure you can care for others over the long haul.

9. **Do a savings and investing checkup**—Are you still on track with your retirement goals?

10. **Consider insurance needs**—Research and update your life, LTC, home, and auto insurance policies.

It's time to start thinking about what your ideal retirement would look like to ensure your retirement transition is a breeze. There's so much to plan for when you hit five years prior to retirement that we've broken this topic into two chapters. The next chapter focuses on preplanning your retirement lifestyle, and the following chapter focuses on preplanning your retirement finances.

Five Years Out: Preplanning Your Retirement Lifestyle

A T SOME POINT, thoughts of retirement will begin to drift through your mind. These thoughts might start a decade before your planned retirement date or pop into your head at your retirement party when coworkers ask, "So, what's next for you?"

> **BIG TIP:** Start visualizing the retirement you want five years before you plan to retire. Be ready to answer those party guests' questions. Waiting until the last minute adds a lot of angst to a major life transition that's stressful by definition.

Why not do your in-depth planning sooner? Many things change on the retirement scene, from Social Security payout amounts to hot trends in retirement communities. So, other than starting to save for retirement as early as possible, as we've discussed, it's not productive to plan much farther out than five years.

Five years before your retirement date is a great time to start figuring out whether your retirement will be an easy transition to a vibrant, well-funded Third Act or whether a meager retirement lifestyle awaits you at the bottom of a long chute. Think of this as a strategic planning stage, where you'll come up with an overall game plan for your post-work life.

Retirement can change your whole life, including where you live, how you access healthcare, how you spend your time, and even how you feel about yourself. You don't want to make major retirement decisions under pressure and at the last minute.

Fortunately, we can offer a lot of guidance to help you understand your retirement situation and make an exciting, yet realistic plan. Now's the time to research your retirement ideas. What you learn may further refine or alter your current ideas.

If you skip early planning, you may seriously regret it. Chris knows because he gave very little attention to preplanning his retirement and waited until age sixty-five to organize his finances as they specifically related to retirement, determine when to take Social Security, and make under-pressure decisions about Medicare. It turned out to be a lot to conquer all at once. He had a ton to learn in a short time, so he could make all the needed decisions. He wishes he had started planning earlier—much earlier.

Now, about five years from retirement, it's time to start your preplanning process! In this preplanning chapter, you'll clarify the *lifestyle* you want in your retirement. In the following preplanning chapter (Chapter 8), you'll estimate your *finances* to see if you can afford the retirement you envision. Next, Chapter 9 will guide you through a greater level of detail—this planning process (as opposed to preplanning) starts about one year from your retirement date.

What's the difference between preplanning and planning? During this preplanning stage, you may consider remaining in your current city and state, retiring to Arizona, or retiring to Florida. Let's say that, after pondering the question of where to live and doing some research, you decide you want to retire to Florida. Congratulations! You just made a major decision in your preplanning stage.

Next, in the planning stage—starting about one year before your retirement date—you'll investigate the realities of the retirement lifestyle you want. For example, you'll select the city in Florida you want to live in and identify the specific property you want to rent or buy. Think of it this way: The preplanning stage is something of an armchair discussion, while the planning stage involves a higher level of detail and decision making.

Early retirement planning is so important that it has acquired a nickname: *pretirement*. Now that so many of us are living longer, our retirement phase is a big chunk of our lives. Do your preplanning now, and you'll have a much easier retirement when the day comes.

Let's dive in, starting with how you'll maintain your health and pay for your healthcare.

How's Your Health?

We meet many people who say they plan to adopt a healthier lifestyle when they retire, but that day never seems to come. Truly, if you're in your fifties or older, realize it's now or never. As we age, we tend to steadily gain weight while steadily losing muscle mass—unless we remain active and keep building our strength and overall fitness.

It will not be easier to get in shape after age sixty, so it's time to get moving. Doctors recommend a regular exercise routine that includes both strength training and aerobic exercise, along with eating a healthy, balanced diet and getting plenty of fluids. Whether you join a health club, hire a trainer, amp up your neighborhood walks, or find steeper bike trails, ask your doctor about ways you can build your strength, endurance, aerobic ability, and overall fitness within any current mobility or health challenges.

Don't be one of those people who say, "I'm sixty now, and it's too late to change" or "I've eaten this way my whole life, and it hasn't killed me."

According to the CDC's 2025 National Diabetes Statistics Report, nearly one-third of Americans have diabetes by age sixty-five. It's sad to see someone who spent their life diligently saving for retirement become ill or disabled in their golden years. They worked hard their entire life, only to be robbed of their chance to enjoy retirement by neglecting their health.

Are you hoping to live your golden years as a vibrant, active senior where you get to enjoy your hard-earned retirement? Then lay the groundwork for good health now. It'll pay rewards for decades to come. And here's a tip—if you're planning a retirement relocation, be sure to research whether your planned move will support your health goals.

A Healthy Place to Live

What are your current and likely future healthcare needs? Be sure to research the quality and availability of healthcare if you plan to relocate. Consider your current health and any conditions that run in your family. Will your retirement location support your well-being in the long run, or could it create new challenges over time?

Speaking of health, be sure to consider the recreational opportunities in your chosen spot. The Environmental Protection Agency presents a National Walkability Index on its website that rates US cities. Check this as well as other opportunities to get out and move, whether you want to hike, bike, play pickleball, or join a bowling league.

> **BIG TIP:** Don't overlook your mental and emotional well-being. Explore whether the community you're considering supports your favorite hobbies and interests. If fly fishing is your passion but there's no fishing scene, you may feel isolated instead of fulfilled.

A healthy retirement starts with a check-in—on both your physical health and what truly brings you joy.

How Many Years Since Your Annual Checkup?

If you've been avoiding the doctor and annual checkups don't exactly happen annually, five years before retirement is a good time to get a complete physical to thoroughly check your health. While you might have skipped checkups when you were younger, regular visits now are crucial to spot potential issues. Remember, early detection saves lives.

You need to know your baseline as you seek to get healthy or stay healthy. Most healthcare plans cover preventive care, such as an annual physical, at 100 percent, so there's no excuse. Get on with it!

It's important to think about safe activities as you age. Feeling young and energetic doesn't mean you should take risks, such as using a swivel chair to change a light bulb. Be aware of your limits to avoid health setbacks. Too many people have faced surgeries and financial losses due to avoidable injuries—a tumble down a serious chute in later life.

Having baseline data about your health status will be important when your health insurance changes. And it's going to.

Medicare: Myths Meet Reality

At sixty-five, Americans are eligible for Medicare. The best time to learn about Medicare is several years before that. Why? You may think signing up for our national healthcare plan would be simple, but it's actually one of the most confusing and complicated decisions you'll make.

We meet people all the time who think it's free. Bulletin: It's not.

The first thing you should know about Medicare is that, no matter what type of health insurance coverage you have at age sixty-five, you should sign up for Medicare at age sixty-five. Otherwise, you'll pay a lifetime penalty for enrolling late.

Don't wait for someone at Medicare to contact you because no one will. It's on you to go to the Medicare website (www.Medicare.gov) and sign up. It's important to enroll at least a month before you turn sixty-five to give the system time to start your benefits. Also, know that these are individual plans. If you are married, you each choose your own Medicare plan and pay separate premiums.

See why we said planning ahead a few years will help?

As a longtime corporate CEO, Chris thought he was a pretty smart guy. When it came to signing up for Medicare, he was boggled! Don't feel bad if you find Medicare confusing. That's a common response for most of us. To help you understand and navigate retirement healthcare, let's address some Medicare basics, so you can understand your choices.

You can receive Medicare coverage through the Original Medicare program or through a Medicare Advantage plan.

Medicare premiums, co-pays, and coverages change over time, so a thick, annual publication called *Medicare & You* explains each year's plans. It's an overwhelming document, but the certified Medicare insurance agent you choose to work with can help you decipher it.

Further complicating your signup journey, a lot of scammers are lurking out there, looking for anyone who is unschooled in Medicare's ins and outs. That's especially true around the annual Medicare Open Enrollment Period from October 15 to December 7.

How to Avoid Medicare Scams

How can you learn about Medicare, choose the right plan for your situation, and avoid being a victim? By educating yourself.

As with any other situation that involves personal data, never share sensitive information, such as your Social Security number or Medicare number, with anyone who calls you on the phone out of the blue. They may say they're from Medicare, but trust us, they're not. If they send you to a website that doesn't end in .gov, beware. Scammers are just trying to get your personal information, so they can steal your identity.

Only discuss your healthcare by directly contacting Medicare, a Medicare Advantage provider, or a certified Medicare insurance agent. Rely on trusted sources if you need help navigating Medicare. Qualified agencies include Medicare itself, The National Council on Aging, and the State Unit on Aging (SUA) in your state or US territory.

How will you access Medicare? First, you need to understand all its parts.

Pick Your Parts

The Medicare program has multiple parts. Depending on the plan you choose, you will use different parts:

- **Part A**—This covers inpatient hospital, hospice, nursing home, and home healthcare. Most Americans are automatically enrolled in Part A and receive it for free.

- **Part B**—This medical coverage includes doctors, preventive services, medical equipment, and outpatient care. This is the part you must sign up for at sixty-five or pay a lifetime 10 percent penalty. You have to pay a monthly premium for Part B.

- **Part C**—These are Medicare Advantage plans, all-in-one plans that cover Parts A, B, and usually D. They often include additional coverage, such as dental and vision. If you buy a Medicare Advantage plan, you cannot buy Medigap (see below).

- **Part D**—This is optional drug coverage. Part D also has a late-signup penalty, but it's much smaller than the Part B penalty.

- **Supplemental health insurance (Medigap)**— Ten different Medigap plans (Medigap plans A-D, F, G, and K-N) cover various out-of-pocket costs.

Should you go with Original Medicare or a Medicare Advantage plan? Let's take a deep dive into how these two types of plans work. Depending on the state of your health, your financial situation, and your skill with navigating healthcare systems, you may find that one is a far better choice for you. Note that we're not discussing premium costs because those are state regulated, so costs and providers vary from state to state.

Seven Original Medicare Basics

This is Medicare as administered directly by the federal government. It covers Parts A and B. Here are seven key things to know about Original Medicare, based on information on the Medicare website at the time of this writing:

1. **Doctors and hospitals**—You can see any doctor and go to any hospital that accepts Medicare anywhere in the United States and US territories.

2. **Referrals/approvals**—You don't need a referral from a primary care physician to see a specialist or approval to get services or supplies.

3. **Co-pays**—You pay 20 percent coinsurance for Part B-covered services. You can purchase supplemental Medigap insurance if you want insurance to cover some of your out-of-pocket costs.

4. **Premiums**—You pay a monthly premium for Part B and another for Part D if you purchase a Medicare drug plan. (Great news on Part D plans—starting in 2025, out-of-pocket costs for medicines are capped.)

5. **Annual limits (caps)**—There is *no annual limit or cap* on how much you will personally pay for medical services, unless you also buy supplemental Medigap insurance. If you have a major medical calamity, you could be on the hook for hundreds of thousands of dollars. *It's critical to note that, with no annual limit or cap on how much you will personally pay for medical services, you have massive financial exposure with Original Medicare unless you buy Medigap.*

6. **Coverage**—As far as coverage, Medicare's website states: "Original Medicare covers most medically necessary services and supplies in hospitals, doctors' offices, and other healthcare facilities. Original Medicare doesn't cover some services, like routine physical exams, eye exams, and most dental care." It also doesn't cover hearing aids.

7. **Drug coverage**—To get drug coverage, you'd need to separately purchase Medicare Part D and pay a separate premium for it.

And there you have it. Original Medicare makes it easy to get covered care, but you're on the hook for an unlimited sum without Medigap, and you still need to look for eye and dental care.

Now, let's see how Medicare Advantage plans compare.

Seven Medicare Advantage Basics

Many large healthcare companies, especially health management organizations (HMOs), want Medicare patients' business. They strive to create competitive Medicare Advantage plans, usually by adding some extra services or features that Original Medicare lacks, hence the Advantage name.

Here is what Medicare Advantage plans offer at the time of this writing, following the same points as above:

1. **Doctors and hospitals**—You'll typically need to use their in-network doctors and hospitals. If you're using an HMO for healthcare now, this will be a familiar setup.

2. **Referrals/approvals**—You may need a referral from your primary care physician to see a specialist or plan approval for certain services and supplies.

3. **Co-pays**—Your out-of-pocket coinsurance or co-pay requirement will vary, but it will often be less than Original Medicare's 20 percent. You can't get Medigap to cover the difference, though.

4. **Premiums**—In addition to the Part B premium you pay directly to Medicare, you may also pay a premium to your Medicare Advantage plan (although many offer a zero-premium option; with these plans you pay no additional premiums, just the Part B premium).

5. **Annual limits (caps)**—Advantage plans have a cap or yearly limit on how much you could be asked to pay for out-of-pocket costs. The amount depends on the plan you choose. If you reach your

annual limit, you pay nothing more for the rest of the year. You cannot purchase Medigap, but you don't need it.

6. **Coverage**—Advantage plans must cover everything Original Medicare does, and they often add more coverage, including dental, eye care, and hearing aids.

7. **Drug coverage**—Medicare Advantage plans often include drug coverage. If so, there's no need to buy Part D separately.

BIG TIP: As you can see, each type of plan has its own pros and cons. *As we mentioned, it's critical to note that, with Original Medicare, you have massive financial exposure unless you buy yet another insurance policy (Medigap).* Original Medicare's major advantage is that it offers far more flexibility in your care. With Medicare Advantage, you must seek approvals and referrals from your providers, but you enjoy a cap on out-of-pocket expenses and usually have more coverage.

It's a daunting task to learn about all the Medicare options and select the plan (or combination of plans) that will best support your financial situation and current state of health. Yes, learning all the ins and outs is a difficult undertaking, but without question, it's a must. Two people we know are facing an incredible challenge because they didn't move forward with Medicare Part B, Medigap, or a Medicare Advantage plan.

Pete and Shirley entered retirement with meager savings. Recently, they received terrible news: Pete was diagnosed with stage IV cancer. Their adult daughter, Deeanna, flew to their city and immediately dug into their financial situation and healthcare coverage.

She found that Pete was receiving Medicare Part A. This Medicare coverage is free to most Americans and provides coverage for inpatient hospital, hospice, nursing home, and home healthcare. To her horror, she discovered that Pete had not purchased Medicare Part B, Medigap, or a Medicare Advantage plan. He has no healthcare coverage for doctor visits, diagnostic tests, medical equipment, and outpatient care. As a result, he's unlikely to get the best care available, given that he's only minimally insured. Worse, Pete and Shirley could incur growing debt throughout his battle with cancer. When she is widowed, Shirley could be burdened by insurmountable debt for the rest of her life.

Compounding the situation, Deeanna discovered that Pete did not have a will, trust, or advance directive (living will). She hired an estate attorney, and the family is moving forward with this important activity.

Pete's lack of preparation created something of a Pandora's box for Shirley, Deanna, and other heirs. Ideally, retired parents ensure they have enough healthcare coverage, prepare their important paperwork, and share all the information with their adult children, so they will have direction and clarity if a similar situation occurs.

How to Choose Your Medicare Plan

As you approach age sixty-five, you'll start to hear from Medicare marketers. You'll get mailers and notice TV ads featuring well-known actors who offer various freebies if you sign up. Clearly, you need to select and purchase a plan, so you don't end up in dire straits like Pete and Shirley. But how do you choose?

> **BIG TIP:** Don't decide on your Medicare plan based on a TV ad! Instead, find a certified Medicare insurance agent or consult an impartial certified Medicare specialist at a government or nonprofit agency who can help you compare plans and choose the best one for your situation. That agent should be familiar with many companies and plans in your state, not just one or a few.

To decide on a plan, Chris met with a certified Medicare insurance representative (and yes, you want to look for that certification). If you've had company insurance all your life, you'll encounter a big learning curve here.

His rep walked him through Medicare Parts A and B and their costs, which vary depending on your income. Costs change each year, so your rep will give you the current rates.

The rep also introduced him to Part D, which he wasn't aware of. Surprise—basic Medicare does not cover medication! Chris didn't feel he needed Part D at that point. However, if he is diagnosed with an illness that requires an expensive drug, he'll have to pay out of pocket for that drug until the next annual Open Enrollment Period, his next opportunity to sign up for Part D. But he sees this as a risk worth taking as it would not be a long wait.

As we mentioned, you will incur a lifetime penalty if you don't sign up for Part D right away, unless you are in Medicare's low-income Extra Help program. When Chris ran the calculations, the penalty seemed small, and he would be able to pay it, but you may feel differently.

Part C (Medicare Advantage plans) limits your choices of locations and doctors. Chris was uncomfortable with these limitations, so his choice was Original Medicare.

Since you're on the hook for 20 percent co-pays with Original Medicare, along with no annual limit for how much you can personally pay for medical expenses, Chris's rep guided him through the options to purchase supplemental insurance (Medigap). Supplemental insurance was more expensive—about $100 a month more—than choosing a Medicare Advantage plan. But it offered better choices, which was important to him.

After meeting with his rep, Chris ended up circling back as he realized he still didn't have dental coverage, which is not covered under Original Medicare. You can see how important it is to ask lots of questions to avoid coverage gaps.

Once you understand how Medicare plans differ, weigh how much healthcare you think you'll need, your financial resources to cover co-pays and deductibles, and how difficult and stressful you may find it to obtain insurer approvals and referrals. Think about how you use healthcare and be sure to ask for pro help. Couples may want to meet with a Medicare insurance rep together, so you can ask more questions, discuss the many options, and determine which plan works best for the person turning sixty-five as well as for the household budget.

Our friend Cindy in Seattle spent over an hour with a Medicare Advantage specialist at her longtime HMO. The specialist asked dozens of questions about her health habits, the healthcare services she uses annually, and medications. The conclusion? As a healthy person, she would pay the least on a zero-premium Medicare Advantage plan, even though this plan carried a higher annual cap than the HMO's premium-paying plans.

Cindy's choice came as a surprise to her husband, who is also healthy. He had previously reviewed these Medicare Advantage plans on his own and had chosen their HMO's highest premium Advantage plan for himself. They're now reviewing his policy to see if they should switch to the zero-premium plan.

This couple was happy to get on Medicare because they'd been self-insured through Cindy's business for decades. They were getting minimal HMO coverage while paying high premiums with an individual plan. If you're wondering, the national average cost is now over $25,000 for a year of self-insured family coverage and nearly $9,000 for an individual—startling figures revealed in the Kauffman Family Foundation's 2024 Employer Health Benefits Survey.

On the other hand, if you've had high-quality, low-cost health insurance through your company, switching to

Medicare may mean higher premium costs and less robust coverage.

When you start Medicare, you may still have other health insurance. You—or a spouse or domestic partner whose plan covers you—may work past age sixty-five. You may also be on COBRA (a continuation of health-care from a previous employer) or elect to continue to be self-insured. Let's look at how Medicare works with these other healthcare plans.

Medicare Plus Other Insurance

When you retire, any company-sponsored health insur-ance you had will end. Planning to work past sixty-five? Nearly one-fifth of us do, according to a 2024 Axios article. You can keep the company or private insurance you have while on Medicare but proceed carefully. If you don't sign up for Medicare, you're in for a rude awaken-ing: Your other healthcare plan will stop paying. Once you're sixty-five, your other plan expects Medicare to pay many of your medical bills, and it will pick up any remaining difference.

It's important to know that if you have multiple possible insurance payers Medicare is in "first position." Confused? Fortunately, the Medicare website has an info page on how Medicare works with other insurance.

Wealthy Retiree? Meet IRMAA

If you expect to have a high income in retirement, you have another cost to watch out for. It's an extra Medicare charge called *income-related monthly adjustment amount* (IRMAA). In our research, we found that roughly 7 to 8 percent of

Medicare recipients pay this extra charge. It affects both Original Medicare and Medicare Advantage plans and is a surcharge that increases what you pay for Medicare parts B and D. Translation: If you're rolling in dough, Uncle Sam will make you pay more for Medicare. The amounts vary by tax bracket and are adjusted annually. To avoid paying IRMAA, you'd have to find ways to lower your adjusted gross income.

As you can see, Medicare is complex enough to drive you crazy. And once you figure it out, you still have decisions to make during the annual Open Enrollment Period if you're considering switching plans.

Your Medicare decisions will be guided, in part, by where you decide to live in retirement and the available healthcare options there. And where you live—like many of the retirement decisions you'll make—will be guided by your values.

Set Your Retirement Priorities

Think about the values that have guided you up until now. Whether your values have changed or not, those core beliefs should shape your retirement decisions. Is family your top priority? Maybe your retirement plan is to relocate to be near grandkids or other relatives. Perhaps you want to live where you can be close to nature and give back to the community by volunteering to support a beloved bay or nature preserve. Once you've clarified how your values impact your retirement plan, it's time to share those ideas with your partner if you're in a relationship.

If you discover areas where your values don't align, start discussing a compromise. If you've known couples who've ended up splitting when they retired, it was probably because they had different visions for their retirement life. Perhaps one wanted to retire to a rural community, and the other wanted to live close to grandkids in a big city. One of the biggest decisions you'll make as you head toward retirement is where you want to live.

How to Pick a Place

The question of retirement location isn't just about picking the best city or town for seniors. It's also about what type and size home you want. Is your dream a rural farmhouse on sprawling acreage or a patio home in a fifty-five-only urban community? This is a much more important choice than you may think. When you visualize your retirement location, think about it from every angle, right down to the coffee shop you can walk to or the availability of close neighbors.

When you envision your retirement, where do you see yourself? Start researching your retirement living options. There's a lot to discover in any prospective relocation locale, from housing prices and recreation opportunities to available natural and cultural resources.

As we write this, retiring abroad is spiking in popularity. And while retirees historically have downsized to a smaller place, these days some "upsize" to a bigger home.

The most popular retirement home in America is the one you're already living in. According to a 2024 article in *Forbes* magazine, more than three-quarters of Americans over fifty don't want to move to a new place or start over in a new town. We feel happier and safer in familiar places.

Staying in the family home may seem like the most affordable option, especially if you own your home free and clear. But realize it may need a major remodel as you age, and be sure to budget for that cost. Over time, you might add a wheelchair ramp, an electric stairlift or elevator, widened hallways and doorways, and more. Downsizing to a one-story house designed for older adults may end up as both a safer and lower-cost option. Do the math.

Another consideration is whether your retirement locale will help you stay healthy. Be sure to research the quality and availability of healthcare if you plan to relocate. A friend's experience offers a good case in point.

———— ☕ ————

Our friend Emily is a breast cancer survivor. She and her husband retired to Las Vegas to be near family but discovered the quality of healthcare in Sin City wasn't up to her standards. She now flies back monthly to the bigger city where they previously lived for all her medical appointments, an extra expense she and her husband never imagined they would incur in their retirement years.

During your preplanning stage, take the time to research everything from recreational activities to restaurants to healthcare and airport locations to ensure your new location is a good fit. Consider renting a place for a few weeks or months and living there as something of a test drive. You'll know if you like the new location soon enough. Chris did this when looking to buy a home at high altitude. He rented a place for two weeks and brought the family there to make sure everyone could acclimate and enjoy themselves when visiting.

Find Your Purpose

While writing this book, we have found ourselves returning to one topic again and again: *purpose*. Nearly every time our book comes up in conversation so does the importance of having a deeper sense of meaning in your life. We've come to realize that purpose isn't just a handy addition to retirement—it's as essential as physical health. In many ways, it's the health of your soul.

Finding purpose isn't just a nice idea—it's the key to a fulfilling life, especially in retirement. When your career winds down and your daily routine shifts, having a strong sense of purpose keeps you engaged, motivated, and thriving.

Purpose gives you a reason to get up in the morning, whether it's pursuing your passion, contributing to your community, or deepening relationships. Without it, retirement can feel aimless rather than rewarding.

The happiest, healthiest retirees are those who stay curious, connected, and committed to something bigger than themselves. What will give your retirement meaning?

Interestingly, women seem to be better at finding their purpose in retirement. But finding purpose is also extremely important for men heading into retirement. In our research, we've found that men who are busy with their careers often have fewer friends than women—and the COVID-19 pandemic made the problem worse. In its 2021 study, the Survey Center on American Life found that five times as many men reported they had *no friends* in 2020 than those who responded to the survey in 1990. This situation can grow into a real issue for men who don't have a meaningful purpose in retirement.

Another factor: Men who had a brilliant professional career or founded a business generally derived high satisfaction from their work. People who didn't love their jobs may be relieved to be done working, but men who loved their work often struggle in retirement. Colleagues looked up to them, and they felt respected. This positive socialization was a source of good mental health.

For these men, their work was their identity and the primary driver of their sense of self-worth. When they retire, that's gone. And navigating a major identity change isn't something our society trains men for.

Complicating matters, men tend to have more health problems than women when they hit sixty-five. Ending up retired in poor physical and mental health slides you into a sad scene. So, let's talk about how to avoid this distressing, downward chute.

Here's our question for *you*: How can you move into retirement feeling great about your life?

BIG TIP: In this preplanning stage, start exploring what will replace work in your retirement years and will give you an ongoing sense of fulfillment and purpose.

As it happens, researchers have identified the critical factors that prevent depression or impaired mental function in retirement. A 2018 article published by the National Institutes of Health discusses psychological well-being in retirement. Researchers found that happy retirees possessed six factors as they approached retirement age:

1. **Self-acceptance**—You're happy in your skin.

2. **Pursuit of personal growth**—You still enjoy learning new things.

3. **Purpose in life**—You've got a reason to get up in the morning.

4. **Positive relations with others**—You get along with those close to you.

5. **Control over your environment**—You have the resources to live where you want.

6. **Ability to make independent decisions**—Your brain is still sharp, and you're in charge of your life.

Let's take a closer look. The researchers identified some concrete examples of these principles, including:

- **Closeness with your partner**—Intimacy is a key to happiness.

- **More social contacts and involvement in social groups**—Friends and activities are important for mental health.

- **Higher income and net assets**—You have enough money to give you control over your environment.

- **Tenacity and flexibility in pursuing goals**—You persist in pursuing your purpose and can shift gears if needed.

- **Your work's importance and job satisfaction levels**—People tend to be happier in retirement if they left a job they didn't love and didn't attach as much self-esteem to the job as, say, a corporate executive might.

- **Your health and your spouse's health**—Health problems can lead to worry and unhappiness, but when you've got your health, life is good. (Now you know why we've been talking about physical and mental health in a retirement book!)

To be happy in retirement, you need to like yourself, stay healthy, have a social life, and feel that your life has purpose. Many people need to find a new purpose in retirement to stay mentally strong.

Our Retirement Purpose

Want to know what we're doing in retirement? Chris readily admits that part of his solution to the retired CEO challenge was writing this book. He loves to mentor people and volunteer, but sharing this practical and important information takes his purpose to another level.

As he reached retirement and saw how difficult the transition was for him, he discovered a passion for helping others retire happy, healthy, and wealthy.

He is already doing public speaking about this book's retirement planning principles and giving more people the insights they need to plan a retirement they love. He enjoys traveling the world with Tracy, especially as a professional speaker. The effort required is far less than the long hours he put in as a hard-driving CEO and is extremely rewarding. Also, he enjoys teaching this topic because he knows he's making a positive contribution to society—and he discovered he needs that.

Like Chris, Tracy believes writing this book has become a powerful part of her purpose. She has always found joy in helping others, and that joy is deeply rooted in supporting other women. She is passionate about helping women of all ages avoid the confusion and lack of information she faced, especially when it comes to investing and planning for the future.

Plus, she views this book as much more than a coauthoring project with Chris—it's a meaningful step into the next chapter of their shared lives as partners. Tracy adds that, through this book, she and Chris have reflected on their shared journey and have used the writing process as a catalyst to plan their next five years with intention. That has been exciting, she says, not scary or uncertain as life often can be when you don't have a plan.

She hopes readers take away this message: Planning is power. And retirement isn't the end but an incredible gift of a new beginning. You just need to change your perspective on what this can mean for you and your family.

Your top ten list for preplanning your retirement is at the end of the next chapter because it continues our preplanning journey, this time with a focus on your retirement finances.

Five Years Out:
Preplanning Your
Retirement Finances

WHEN YOU RETIRE, the paycheck-driven life you've
known will end. At that time, you will receive pas-
sive income from your retirement accounts and, possibly,
monthly Social Security checks. This is the ladder you've
been building all your life that will support your lifestyle
in your later years.

How much income will you have? Estimate it now.
Don't wait until you're in the process of retiring to figure
it out. Typical sources of retirement income include:

- Social Security
- Corporate pension or charitable organization
  distributions
- Individual retirement accounts (IRAs)
- Roth IRAs
- 401(k) plan withdrawals
- Brokerage or investment accounts

- Investment income
- Annuity payouts
- Rental income
- Part-time job
- Sale of other assets, such as fine art, collectibles, or jewelry

We'll discuss these income sources one at a time to help you estimate your income. But first, look up your current tax bracket and think about how that might change when you retire. Your choices can give you a fairly tax-free retirement with more spending money, or you can find much of your hard-earned money going to the taxman. In other words, how you save for retirement matters. Now's the time to think about your retirement taxes while you still have time to make changes.

How Much Will You Pay the Taxman?

If you're like most people, you'd like to pay as little tax as possible when you retire. Every dollar will be precious. One of the simplest ways to do this is by minimizing your taxable income. You want to avoid paying as much tax as you legally can as a retiree.

You may have the impression that your tax rate will be lower once you stop working. For generations, financial advisors told us to make tax-free retirement deposits into IRAs and 401(k)s. The reasoning for this advice? During your working life, your income is higher than it will be in retirement. And so is your tax bracket. Avoid higher taxes now, in your working years, and you'll likely have a lower income in retirement and will pay lower taxes on your withdrawals. That was the theory.

But will you *really* pay lower taxes in retirement? That's the big question. It may depend on whether your retirement income will be small or large. Of course, if you're living a low-income retirement, you may pay very little to no tax.

Financial experts are discussing (and disagreeing on) an even bigger issue—the question of future tax rates. It's important for anyone who expects a moderate-to-high retirement income to know about this issue. You can calculate your retirement income and learn if it will be lower, higher, or the same as your working income based on today's tax rates. But here's the mystery: No one knows what will happen to federal tax rates in the future.

A growing school of thought holds that US tax rates simply must rise at some point as our nation reckons with its massive government debt. Our tax rates were much higher in the past—in fact, the top tax rate was 94 percent in 1944! (A handy chart on the Wolters Kluer website offers a fascinating view of historical income tax rates.)

If tax rates do jump, you might pay higher taxes in retirement than you do now. That is, unless you figure out ways to reduce your taxable retirement income to keep yourself in a lower tax bracket. (The section below on Roth IRAs discusses a tax-cutting strategy.) If you have substantial retirement assets, you should talk with a tax advisor to plan your best course of action. Unless you're planning to spend your free time tracking new tax laws and tax-rate changes, meeting with a tax advisor really is a must. This is a small investment of your time and money that can pay off in vastly reduced tax bills during your retirement years.

One of the top ways early tax planning can really pay off is by helping you avoid paying taxes on your Social Security income. So, let's look at this income source first.

Social Security: Make Informed Decisions

In talking with people as we researched this book, we were shocked to discover widespread ignorance about how Social Security works. This surprised us because it's easy to find out what your monthly Social Security payment will be when you decide to retire and receive your benefits.

Set up an account on the Social Security Administration website (www.SSA.gov) to view your annual statements online. These informative statements show your income for up to thirty-five working years, along with your projected benefit at various ages, such as sixty-two, sixty-five, and seventy. The SSA website has a handy retirement checklist, along with information about how to claim and maximize your benefit.

The age at which your Social Security benefit kicks in depends on your birth year. Most Boomers can start receiving Social Security at age sixty-two, but your benefit keeps growing until age seventy if you delay taking it until then. Sadly, many Americans can't afford to wait or simply don't understand the consequences of taking Social Security early. In our research, we found that about 30 percent of Americans claim the benefit right away, cutting their payout nearly in half compared to waiting until age seventy.

If you live a long life, the difference could easily add up to tens of thousands of dollars, perhaps even hundreds of thousands of dollars, of lost income. Think about your current health and your genetics. When did your grandparents and parents die, or are they still living at an advanced old age?

With your likely life expectancy in mind, play around with a longevity calculator to see when it makes statistical sense for you to claim your Social Security benefit. You can find longevity calculators online. We found one called the Health Life Expectancy Calendar by the Goldenson Center at the University of Connecticut.

For some, it'll make sense to start taking your benefit at sixty-two. However, for most of us, that would be a costly mistake—a chute representing thousands of dollars in lost income year after year, decade after decade.

One of the best reasons to do preplanning is having time to think about how *other* income sources might pay your bills until your Social Security benefit fully vests. This strategy will help you set yourself up for higher Social Security income for the rest of your life. Some Americans choose to work until age seventy to delay their benefit, for instance.

Craft your own approach, but try to avoid taking Social Security early. Simply waiting to fully vest can be the equivalent of catching up on retirement savings if you haven't put away enough in your retirement savings account.

Your Incredible Shrinking Social Security Check

You've gotten some solid figures from your Social Security Administration statements, but there's something important they don't tell you—what your net income will be

from Social Security. The figures you're seeing aren't the amount you'll keep.

What is taken out of your Social Security check? First, your Medicare premiums will be deducted. The remainder goes to you—until tax time.

That's right. Social Security income is taxable income for many Americans. As of July 4, 2025, a new law allows a standard deduction expansion that reduces federal income tax liability for many, but it is not a repeal of *all* taxes on Social Security. The bottom line? With each administration these laws can vary, making it important to stay up to date for your retirement planning.

Let's do some quick math to see how this pencils out. Let's say Susie has done well in her career and has ample retirement savings, so 85 percent of her Social Security income will be taxed in the top tax bracket. She has also selected an Original Medicare plan plus Medigap. At the time of this writing, here's how her monthly Social Security check works out.

Monthly Social Security benefit:	$4,100
85% ($3,485) taxed at 37%:	($1,289)
Original Medicare premium:	($178)
Medigap:	($217)
Net Social Security benefit:	**$2,416**

That's quite a difference in monthly income, yes? Now, let's run the numbers for John. He hasn't been a saver, and his Social Security benefit is only average, so he won't pay tax on his Social Security income.

Monthly Social Security benefit:	$1,783
Medicare premium for Part B:	($178)
Medicare Advantage premium:	($58)
Net Social Security benefit:	**$1,547**

Obviously, this is a meager amount to live on each month. Bonus points for you if you noticed that hardworking Susie only netted about $870 a month more from Social Security than John due to her higher tax bracket.

During this preplanning stage, you'll want to consider multiple issues around Social Security income, such as how working while taking Social Security will affect your benefit, how and when you should claim your spouse's Social Security benefit instead of yours, and more. Research carefully to understand how to get the most from this income source.

- **Social Security pros**—Benefits are indexed for inflation, so the monthly benefit grows if prices are rising.

- **Social Security cons**—Social Security income is taxable income for most Americans.

This is your money that you paid in to Social Security throughout your working career. Now, you get at least some of it back. And if you don't like the figures you're seeing in your Social Security statements, you still have a few years to work and increase your benefit.

Corporate and Charity Pensions: What to Know

Do you have a pension from a company or nonprofit organization? These are known as *defined benefit plans*. Call your pension plan administrator to learn your projected monthly benefit amount. If you keep working at the same organization for additional years, then that benefit may rise.

- **Pension pros**—Like Social Security, this is a lifetime payout with survivor benefits. And you don't have to figure out how to invest it, the pension managers do that for you.

- **Pension cons**—Most pension income is taxable income. And you have no control over how it's invested over the years.

IRAs and Required Withdrawals

With traditional IRAs, you deposit money tax-free, and it grows tax-free, but you will pay tax in retirement on your withdrawals. You can start withdrawing your IRA money as early as age fifty-nine-and-one-half without penalty. If possible, wait until later, so the money continues to grow.

Once you reach a certain age in your seventies—the exact age depends on your birth year—you must withdraw money each year. These are known as *required minimum distributions* (RMDs). The percentage you must withdraw is based on several factors, including your age and average life expectancy. The withdrawal percentage shrinks as you age, but if your remaining invested money keeps growing, the required payout amount will still rise. (If your primary beneficiary is more than ten years younger than you, the calculations are different.)

Fortunately, you can find free calculators online to help you calculate your RMD. For a quick example, let's say Susie is turning seventy-three in 2024, and that's her first year for RMDs. She has $100,000 in her traditional IRA, and her spouse-beneficiary is a similar age. Susie must withdraw just over $3,773 by April 1 after her seventy-third birthday or pay a whopping tax on the difference.

You may be thinking: "I can't live on that!" Of course you can't. You can withdraw more, but it's not an ideal option because this money needs to last the rest of your life.

That's why it's so important to save more and keep your money invested, so it continues to grow. How much growth can you expect? Investment pros say to expect an average 10 percent return, some of which should be reinvested.

To determine a safe amount for annual withdrawals during retirement, money managers often recommend following the 4 percent rule. If you don't withdraw more than 4 percent of your retirement funds per year, you won't outlast your money if it's invested in a typical, diversified, well-balanced portfolio. More recently, some experts have posited a slightly lower figure for annual withdrawals—3.7 percent instead of 4 percent—given our longer lives, lower investment returns, and rising prices.

Consider what's happened to home insurance prices. It doesn't matter whether you believe climate change is real or not—home insurance companies do, and they're hiking premium prices to cover growing losses from disasters, such as the 2024 Los Angeles fires. That is, when they're willing to continue offering insurance in an affected area at all. This is just one example of how the future may be more costly than we think. All the more reason to save even more than the experts say you'll need.

The math on IRA withdrawals, Social Security, and taxes can be an eye-opener. If you imagined living a great lifestyle between your IRA savings and Social Security benefit, this may motivate you to save more in your final working years.

> **BIG TIP:** If you're over fifty, you can make additional annual "catch-up" deposits into an IRA, beyond the regular maximum amounts. The rules change annually, so look up the amount each year on the IRS website.

- **IRA pros**—Your money has grown tax-free in your traditional IRA account over time.

- **IRA cons**—Traditional IRA withdrawals are taxable income, and this additional income may cause your Social Security benefit to be taxed as well.

Roth IRAs: What the Buzz Is About

Introduced in 1998, Roth accounts are the new kid on the retirement-savings block. Roths come in several flavors, including IRAs, Roth 401(k) plans, and more.

From a tax perspective, Roth accounts are the opposite of traditional IRAs: You pay tax on the money when you deposit it, at your current tax rate. Then, you withdraw funds from the account during your retirement years tax-free.

As a hedge against possible future higher taxes, some well-off people are taking money out of their traditional IRA and transferring it into a Roth IRA. If you do this, you must pay taxes at your current rate on the money you move since you didn't pay taxes on that money when you invested it in your traditional IRA. The money then needs to sit in the Roth IRA for at least five years before you withdraw it, or you'll pay a 10 percent penalty. This is a great example of why retirement preplanning matters. Yes, it can be a major tax bill, which is why many people spread the migration over five years to avoid taking the hit all at once.

If you believe your tax rate will be higher in retirement, you'll save money in the long run with this strategy because you'll have more tax-free income in retirement. This strategy may also help to keep your Social Security income tax-free as well. Be sure to consult a tax pro if you're contemplating a Roth conversion to make sure you do this correctly.

Another Roth move can help cut your retirement tax bill: If you don't need your RMD from your traditional IRA each year because you can live off other income sources, you can roll over the RMD into a Roth IRA account. You pay taxes on the money at that point, possibly at lower tax rates than we'll see in the future, and you can withdraw it tax-free later.

- **Roth pros**—Roth IRAs are exempt from RMD rules, so you can leave your money to grow longer if you like. If your tax rate is low now, making Roth deposits can be painless. And if your tax rate is higher in retirement, you'll be glad you fed a Roth account. As with a traditional IRA, your money grows over time tax-free.

- **Roth cons**—If your tax rate is currently high, you may not want to feed a Roth account and pay income taxes now. Paying taxes now robs you of investment money you could grow over time. And if your tax rate ends up lower in retirement, you'll kick yourself for paying more tax in the years prior to retirement.

By the way, we were aware of many of these IRA facts and discovered more in our research. Given that tax laws can change at any time, be sure to check with your accountant or the IRS website for up-to-date information.

Brokerage or Trading Accounts

If you earn a substantial income or perhaps receive an inheritance or business-sale payout, you may have more cash to invest than you can salt away in tax-sheltered retirement accounts in a single year. In the meantime, you might put that money into a stock-trading account.

Many stock investors don't just buy and hold securities forever. They sell stocks or funds that have grown in value to reinvest the proceeds in other market opportunities. Depending on how long the investor holds that security, these sales create either short-term or long-term gains, also known as *profits*. Because they're not in a tax-sheltered account, these profits are subject to capital gains tax, according to the Capital Gains and Losses web page on the IRS website.

Capital gains tax rates vary by income level and often change. In overview, short-term gains are usually taxed as regular income, while long-term gains are usually taxed at lower capital-gains rates, currently ranging from 15 to 20 percent. Some investors hold stocks for a year before selling, so they'll pay the lower, long-term gains tax.

- **Trading account pros**—You're free to invest in whatever securities you like. You could also use your profits to help fund retirement accounts, moving money out of this taxable account over time into tax-deferred or untaxed vehicles.

- **Trading account cons**—You do pay taxes on gains.

Investment Income Strategies

One often-overlooked retirement income source is the money your investments generate in the accounts you control. Think of dividend-paying stocks, for example. That dividend income is spendable cash that doesn't reduce your core holdings.

Instead, most investors take a buy-and-hold approach. In general, mutual funds don't have much yield, perhaps 2 percent or less. Instead of high income, you're hoping these securities' market value will increase over time. In other words, their stock price will go up. Then, you'll sell some of your securities at a profit to get the money you need to live on.

The problem? This bet on market value may pay off, or it may not. You could retire at a time when stock markets are crashing, and it would be foolish to sell. Then, you're stuck living off Social Security until markets recover.

It gets worse. As you liquidate those assets to pay bills, your assets shrink. That means they will generate less cash in the future. If you keep selling to profit from your market-value gains, eventually your retirement account will be empty. Then, you'll be broke and asking your kids for help.

When you're ready to retire, talk with your financial advisor about possibly switching the focus of your investing from a buy-and-hold approach to generating income.

How does it work? Instead of investing in low-yielding mutual funds, you invest part or all your portfolio in securities that pay investors high yields per share every month or quarter. Two examples include individual stocks of companies that pay fat dividends or high-yielding exchange-traded funds.

With income-focused investing, your account might earn enough monthly to cover your bills while keeping your entire retirement nest egg intact. When you talk with your advisor, see if they can help you with this strategy.

- **Income investing pros**—You preserve your assets, so they keep generating income. They should last as long as you live and can be inherited by your heirs.

- **Income investing cons**—Investment income is taxable income. Most investors are less familiar with this approach and need education or pro help to create a well-balanced, diversified, high-yield, income-focused portfolio.

Annuities: Proceed with Caution

Are you expecting a small Social Security benefit, but you've done better in later years? Maybe you've received an inheritance or gotten a big promotion with a salary increase. If you lack other substantial income streams, you may want to consider an annuity.

The joke about annuities is that they are both simple and complex. With the simple kind of annuity, you give an insurer a lump sum of cash, and they give you a guaranteed monthly payout for life.

More complex annuities come with customized guarantees. You can choose one where payouts last ten years, even if you die sooner, for instance, or a joint annuity where payouts continue as long as either spouse lives.

A deferred annuity doesn't start paying out right away. These are sometimes referred to as *longevity insurance*. Payouts kick in when you're older, at a time when other retirement-income sources may be running low.

- **Annuity pros**—You receive predictable monthly income for the rest of your life. You can tailor complex annuities to fit your needs.

- **Annuity cons**—You no longer have access to your money, and there's some interest-rate risk since you lock in at current rates when you buy. Also, your heirs don't inherit anything. The payments stop when you die in a classic annuity. Watch out for early-withdrawal penalties and high fees. If you die before a deferred annuity starts paying out, your heirs receive nothing.

Many financial advisors don't love annuities, and they're complex products to understand. If you've maxed out all your other options and are looking for reliable income, consider discussing annuities with your advisor.

Milking the Cash Cow of Rental Property

Many people who dislike stock market investing put their money into rental property. As you near retirement, it's time to evaluate your rental property to decide if you want to continue owning it or if you want to cash out.

If your property has appreciated, selling could generate a lump sum of cash you could invest in other ways. Perhaps you see expensive maintenance costs coming up, such as roofing and plumbing upgrades, and want to sell now rather than take the financial hit.

On the other hand, perhaps your properties are paid off, are in good condition, and are paying lucrative rents. In that case, rents could offer a great source of reliable monthly income—the kind that can help you put off taking Social Security until age seventy.

- **Rental pros**—You're building equity while you own property. Also, all the property repairs and upgrades are a tax write-off.

- **Rental cons**—Rental income is taxed as regular income. So, if you have a high income, your tax rate on this income will also be high.

Other Income

You may have a few other sources of income. Perhaps you receive royalties or licensing fees from intellectual property you created or income from the sale of collectibles, for instance. If so, add that income to your list. During this preplanning stage, estimate all your retirement income sources and add them up. Are you happy with the total? If not, you still have time to make changes.

Does It Add Up to Enough?

Now you can add up all your anticipated annual income and compare it to the estimated cost of the retirement you want. Is there a shortfall? There usually is. Working people over sixty-five are often trying to fill that gap.

How do your figures compare with typical retirement income and spending? In our research, we found that the average US retirement income is $75,000, while average spending is nearly $58,000, according to a Motley Fool article titled "This Is the Average Income for Retirees in America." If this describes your situation, pat yourself on the back. You're a good saver and have left plenty of wiggle room for unexpected expenses.

If your retirement income is lower than you want, let's figure out how to close the gap by building an estimated retirement budget. Comparing this projected budget with your current household budget may be an eye-opener, and it gives you useful information for decision-making. If you're short, you face some hard choices. Find ways to save more now or scale back your retirement plan.

The Price Tag of Your Golden Years

What will your basic retirement costs be? It's time to come up with an estimate. Costs will probably include a number of items, such as:

- Moving, home purchase, or remodeling costs
- Healthcare costs in your planned location
- Your travel budget
- Taxes and insurance
- Basic living expenses, such as food, utilities, and transportation-related costs
- Emergency fund
- Restaurants and entertainment

Doing this exercise during your preplanning stage will help you discover if there's a shortfall *now*, not during your retirement years. Run what-if scenarios for staying put and relocating. What if you rent a new place and invest the proceeds from the sale of your current home? What if you move in with your grown kid's family? It's time to find out if the ladder you've built reaches your desired retirement destination or if it's a few rungs short.

Here's another consideration when you calculate your retirement income: Are you planning to use up your assets or preserve them?

Some people want to live off their investment income in retirement and leave some or all their savings for their heirs to inherit. If so, you'll have less spending money in retirement than if you plan to spend it all and die broke. Do you have this choice? Run the numbers to see if you could live on income alone or if you must consume assets to stay afloat.

Achieving Balance

If your projected retirement budget doesn't balance, take a look at your current budget. You can take steps now in this preplanning stage to balance your retirement budget. Here are some ideas:

- Scale back your planned retirement lifestyle.
- Work harder now to save more.
- Cut current expenses to save more.
- Invest more aggressively now to earn more.

Since we meet few people who are interested in starving as retirees, let's focus on saving more money now. That means working harder, cutting expenses, taking on more investment risk, or pursuing a mix of these strategies.

Fifteen Ways to Save More

If you're earning all you can, then the only way to save more is to cut expenses. Here's a brainstorming list of cost-cutting ideas for a typical middle-class family as the adults near age sixty:

1. Have just one family car instead of two. Or take transit—cars are expensive!
2. Downsize to a more affordable house or community.
3. Sell your house, invest the proceeds, and rent instead of owning.
4. Rent out a spare room.

5. Cut back on food deliveries and meals out.

6. Grocery shop less frequently and strictly adhere to a list to cut impulse purchases.

7. Eliminate the latte stops.

8. Clean your own house.

9. Do your own yard work.

10. Hunt and kill obsolete subscriptions.

11. Investigate how to cut prescription drug costs.

12. Scrutinize medical bills and push back on questionable charges.

13. Rebid your insurance policies and find more affordable providers.

14. Got a pet? Get pet insurance to guard against expensive health issues.

15. Stop paying adult kids' expenses.

Make moves like these, and you may be amazed at how much you can save month after month. Be creative: Chris reviewed one family member's medication costs and was able to save them $300 a month by helping them switch to generics and eliminate unnecessary and ineffective medications. If you have a family member with many medications, repeat this review process regularly.

> **BIG TIP:** At this point in the game, it's probably too late to find cheap long-term care insurance, but check to see if you can find an affordable plan. It will only be more expensive at sixty-five, and LTC insurance can save you a fortune if the worst happens.

If you can't earn more or cut expenses, consider taking more investment risk in the hope that your money will grow faster.

Time to Check Your Investment Risk

Have you been playing it too safe with your investments? If so, a financial advisor can help you rebalance your portfolio to generate more returns on a five- to ten-year time frame. At this point, we hope you have an ongoing relationship with an advisor who knows your preferences and can steer you to securities that would fit your short-term growth goals.

Don't do anything crazy! If your chosen investments sink in value, you no longer have twenty to thirty years for them to recover. Yes, compound interest will do less for you at this point, but it can still make a difference.

Also, don't ditch your advisor unless you are a skilled, knowledgeable investor because that move can backfire. It's risky unless you're a trained pro, as Maggie's story illustrates.

———————— ☕ ————————

Tracy recently dined out with her friend, Maggie. A single, retired architect who lives in Utah, Maggie said she had stopped working with her advisor to manage her own money. She felt she had overpaid for the advisement services and had gotten lackluster results.

What happened? She made some changes to her portfolio without understanding the tax consequences and ended up owing the IRS $10,000! She saved some money in advisor *fees, but she paid much more in taxes. Maggie needs to either retain a pro on a consulting basis for occasional check-ins or learn more about investing and tax implications before taking on all the investment responsibilities herself.*

A percentage point of gain on your investments one way or the other can make a big difference at this point in your preretirement years. It could mean the difference between having a travel budget in retirement or not. And many retirees want to travel—a lot.

A Trip or Two or Three

Quick quiz: Would you rather travel often in retirement or retire to a huge house in your dream location? These are some of the retirement tradeoffs to think about during this preplanning stage.

For some retirees, travel costs can be one of their biggest retirement expenses. Other folks traveled a lot in their youth and are ready to plop into that front-porch rocking chair. You may be at one of those two poles or somewhere in between.

Investment advisors often think in terms of three levels of travel planning:

- **Go-go**—You want to see the world!

- **Slow-go**—You want to travel but not constantly, perhaps due to budget constraints or physical limitations.

- **No-go**—You're a homebody, are no longer able to travel, or have already been there, done that.

Many people progress through these categories as they age. Travel is hard on our bodies due to jet lag, new foods, unfamiliar environments, and less control over our schedule. One day, you ask distant family members to come visit you rather than going to visit them.

Estimate how many years you might spend in each of these categories. If you plan to travel, price a few trips to get a realistic idea of costs and add this line item to your retirement budget.

The preplanning outlined in this chapter is your chance to go from dreaming about your retirement scenario to creating a more concrete overview of what you can realistically afford. Now that you have this data, you have a few years to increase your retirement investments and, if you plan to spend time in the go-go travel category, build a fat vacation fund.

Top Ten Takeaways for Retirement Preplanning

What are the most important things for you to plan five years ahead to create a smooth road to a healthy, wealthy retirement with purpose? Here are our top tips regarding your retirement lifestyle and finances:

1. **Learn about Medicare**—It's complicated, and you will have many choices for many different programs.

2. **Size up Social Security**—Learn what your net monthly benefit will be after taxes and Medicare premiums. If you can, earn more in your remaining work years to increase your Social Security benefit.

3. **Reevaluate your values**—What will be important to you? Design a retirement plan that reflects those values.

4. **Think about your purpose**—What will you do in retirement that makes you excited to get out of bed in the morning?

5. **Consider where to live**—Start researching possible retirement locations that offer the healthcare and physical activities you want or estimate remodeling costs to age in place.

6. **Estimate your retirement income**—Assess all income sources and add up the numbers.

7. **Estimate retirement costs**—What will your expenses be?

8. **Create a retirement budget**—Compare anticipated income and costs to see if you can afford the lifestyle you want.

9. **Learn about future taxes**—Strategize with a financial advisor to determine if your retirement-era tax rate may be higher or lower.

10. **Brainstorm the balance**—Think about moves you could make now to improve your post-sixty-five financial picture.

Yes, you have a lot of preplanning tasks to address to create an easy transition to your retirement. That's why we want you to start preplanning five years before you retire. Time flies, and your retirement date will arrive before you know it!

One Year to Go: Firming Up Your Retirement Plan

IN YOUR PREPLANNING stage starting five years before retirement, you began to think strategically about your retirement lifestyle and finances. Now, retirement is staring you in the face, and that transition will happen in the next year.

It's time to research more thoroughly and narrow down your plans to the exact retirement scenario you want and can afford. We're moving from general strategy to specific tactics to ensure you're ready for a smooth retirement transition. It's nice to know you're near the top of the retirement ladder you've been climbing!

Let's revisit the difference between preplanning and planning. In your preplanning stage, you may have decided you want to retire to Florida. In this more decisive planning stage, you'll select the city in Florida you want to live in, identify your favorite neighborhood, and find the specific property you want to rent or buy. While your preplanning was something of an armchair discussion,

your action-packed planning stage will involve finalizing your plan by getting out and investigating the realities of the retirement lifestyle you want. Does it measure up to what you imagined, or does it fall short?

In this chapter, we'll revisit all the topics we've been discussing—money, health, values, and purpose—and take them to a new level. It's time to bring the details of your retirement plan into focus. It all starts with getting the real numbers on your retirement income. That way, you won't waste time on plans that can't work for you. Let's get to work finalizing plans for a Third Act you'll love and that's within your means.

Ten Questions to Find All Your Retirement Money

If you stepped through our two preplanning chapters, we hope you calculated your retirement income. If you're near (or at) your retirement age and didn't preplan, we encourage you to read the previous two chapters, which focus on preplanning your lifestyle and preplanning your finances, to learn more about key retirement decisions, especially those having to do with Medicare and Social Security.

Now, it's time to update those numbers and find out exactly what you'll receive each month as you shift from relying on paychecks or business income to living off savings and Social Security.

Here are some questions to help you calculate your monthly income during retirement:

1. Are you 100 percent retiring, or will you still work a part-time job? Estimate any net after-tax employment income.

2. When will you take Social Security? Can you wait until your full vesting age to get the maximum monthly payment? Have you researched when it makes sense for you to take Social Security, based on your family history and likely longevity?

3. Has your Social Security benefit increased since you preplanned? Visit the Social Security Administration's website to check your monthly benefit amount. Additional earned income, waiting until your full vesting age, and cost of living increases can all change your benefit.

4. Have you estimated your net Social Security income after Medicare premiums and taxes are deducted?

5. Do you have retirement accounts, such as traditional IRAs, that are subject to required minimum distributions (RMDs)? If so, how much will you have to withdraw in the first few years? How will that income affect your Social Security taxes?

6. Can you still move retirement money into tax-free vehicles, such as a Roth IRA, to reduce your taxable income and avoid paying tax on your Social Security benefit?

7. What tax bracket do you estimate you'll be in?

8. Is the tax code different in the state you plan to retire to versus your current state?

9. What, if any, monthly pension or other savings account income do you expect?

10. Do you have any other income sources, such as rents or royalty income?

Think through all your income sources and the taxes you expect to pay, based on your total taxable income. You should be able to accurately estimate your monthly retirement income.

Are you coming up short? It may be time to evaluate your investment strategy with a financial advisor. With your retirement date coming up fast, find out if you are investing aggressively enough.

In the past, many advisors would tell retirees to pull most of their stock market holdings in favor of bonds and other conservative strategies. But if you come from a long-lived family, you may want to reconsider that idea. Some of us will be retired for thirty years or more, so it can make sense to keep some money aggressively invested for growth.

We encourage you to meet with your financial advisor to get a projection for making your money last if you live to age ninety, not just the average age forecast on the government's life-expectancy charts.

Your Real Numbers

You have estimated your income and your regular monthly expenses. Does this budget balance? If not, it's time to alter your retirement plan. Your income needs to cover basic expenses, such as healthcare, food, utilities, transportation, and rent or mortgage, before you look at discretionary items. And most retirees would like to enjoy a lifestyle that offers more than the bare basics. Don't forget about all those trips you plan to take!

Also, consider any additional financial needs beyond your living expenses, entertainment, and your travel budget. Do you need to set up a trust to support an adult special needs child for the rest of their life? Perhaps your values call you to fund college costs for a grandchild. If so, include these costs in your retirement budget.

Now that you have real-world income information, you can plan a retirement that fits your budget. That begins with one big decision: Where will you live?

Checklist to Choose a Healthy Retirement Spot

Besides fitting your budget, your retirement locale should check many other boxes. Here's a checklist of factors to consider. Your retirement place should enable you to:

- **Eat healthily**—Do nearby grocery stores offer fresh produce? Can you find healthy options on restaurant menus? Or are you in a health food desert?

- **Do your favorite exercises or activities**—Is it easy for you to do the types of workouts, exercises, or activities you enjoy? Recall our earlier example—if flyfishing is your passion, you will want to retire near a fish-filled stream.

- **Easily access affordable healthcare**—Do quality providers accept Medicare in this location? How far away are the nearest clinics and hospitals? If you're relocating, remember that healthcare is state regulated, so your plan's coverages, premium prices, and facilities could differ widely.

- **Find community**—Whether it's a bowling league, church group, or AA meetings, make sure the support and socializing you need are available in this location.

- **Live your values**—How will your location enable your purpose? Will it be near family, offer appealing volunteer opportunities, have a college where you could take extension courses? If you want to travel a lot, is it near an airport?

- **Enjoy your desired lifestyle**—Whether you want to join a cohousing cooperative, find a fifty-five-plus community with loads of activities, or rent a condo, make sure the community offers the type of home you want.

- **Live within your budget**—If your dream location would quickly drain your savings, it's not a good choice.

As you can see, you will want to investigate many factors if you plan to relocate in retirement. Perhaps the trickiest plan to navigate is aging in place. You may assume retirement will work great in your current neighborhood, but does it have the resources you'll need in older age? It's time to find out.

Start by asking friends if they plan to stay put in retirement or if they're planning to move away. If you want to stay in your current area because "all my friends live nearby," find out if this will continue to be true.

Family, Near or Far

Many retirees often relocate to be closer to their family, particularly to spend more time with grandchildren. The idea of living nearby or even moving in with grown children can seem like a dream—a chance to be more involved in their lives and create lasting memories. However, for many, a layer of denial may surround this decision. The reality of daily proximity may not be as idyllic as it seems.

If your relationship with your children isn't as close as you'd like or if they value their privacy, you may want to reconsider this idea. In such cases, staying where you are and planning regular visits could be a healthier, more realistic option. This allows for connection without overwhelming either party, giving you the space to nurture the relationship while respecting boundaries.

Is Your Dream Locale Really So Dreamy?

Before committing to a major move, look into the resources that would support you in your new locale. Don't throw a pin at a map or rely on a friend's advice. Visit your intended retirement city and ask a lot of questions. For instance, utilities costs vary widely across the country. What will you pay for water, trash removal, electricity, and gas? Property tax rates for your dream home in another state also may be higher.

Drive around the prospective neighborhood, including at night. Do you like what you see and hear? That on-the-ground research can help you avoid a costly mistake. When you're on a limited income, retiring somewhere you don't like and having to move again wastes precious dollars. Here's one example of how this can happen.

———————— ☕ ————————

Our friend, Ryan, who lived in a family-friendly neighborhood in Minneapolis, decided to retire to a spot two hours north of the city. He had visited the area a few times but hadn't taken a deep dive into learning what it might be like to live there permanently.

He chose a ten-unit luxury townhouse complex that had a buzz around it. Several of his friends had investigated the development but ultimately had passed. Ryan thought the small size would create a tight-knit community where he could make new friends. But once he moved in, he quickly realized the reality was very different.

Only a few units are occupied by full-time residents. Seven are used as short-term rentals, so instead of familiar neighbors, he's surrounded by a steady stream of strangers. Ryan didn't think to ask about rental policies before buying. Now, he's living in a beautiful but lonely place that doesn't offer the sense of belonging he was hoping for.

"There's nobody here to make friends with," he told us.

Ryan also didn't research whether this location offered nearby trails or bike paths, which are key to his workouts and mental health. As it turns out, he needs to drive some distance to access a trail. Also, his new place does not have a local coffee shop within walking distance, which was an important and pleasant part of his morning ritual in his old neighborhood.

The final blow? He discovered it's a ninety-minute drive to the nearest doctor. Now, he's depressed, seeing a therapist, and considering moving again.

As Ryan told us about his challenges with this new location, we realized a large part of his story is that he may need to clarify his purpose in this stage of his life—and connect his location and activities to that purpose. We know he enjoys traveling and mountain biking, so perhaps he can ramp up that activity by making more friends in the biking community and traveling to mountain biking meccas in the US. No matter what he chooses, Ryan seems to need more in his retirement, like so many others. You can see why focusing on purpose is crucial to create your joyful retirement.

Peace Is in the Details

Your on-the-ground research in the months before your retirement date will help to create a smooth transition. You have real data on your income and expenses, so you can retire knowing you're able to live within your means. You've checked out how you'll access healthcare in your retirement community. You know what your lifestyle will look like, including who you'll see and how you'll spend your time. And you know how you will enjoy your healthy, wealthy retirement with a clear sense of purpose. (As a reminder, having a purpose in retirement is vital. If you're still struggling to identify what your purpose will be in your retirement years, we encourage you to reread the Find Your Purpose section in Chapter 7.)

The more detailed you can make your retirement plan, the more peace of mind it'll bring you. With a completed plan, you'll come to that retirement party relaxed and ready to tell colleagues about your exciting plans for the future.

Top Seven Takeaways for Your Retirement Year

You're almost there. Follow our tips to make sure you're ready to turn in your work badge and retire shortly:

1. **Calculate your income**—Know how much you'll see monthly from your retirement accounts, Social Security, and other income sources.

2. **Investigate your location choice**—Visit your desired location to learn as much as you can.

3. **Assess resources**—Will you have what you need in your retirement locale?

4. **Talk with family**—If you plan to live near family members, how often should you plan to visit? For example, can you plan a weekly activity with the grandkids?

5. **Calculate expenses**—Be sure to include complete living costs, including utilities and taxes.

6. **Build your retirement budget**—Can you afford the lifestyle you've planned, including travel?

7. **Don't forget family needs**—Know your boundaries and desires when it comes to helping kids and grandkids with education and more.

Now that you've completed your on-the-ground research, you should be ready to make the leap from worker bee to retiree with confidence.

Welcome to Your Healthy, Wealthy Retirement!

You've finally made it: Your retirement date has arrived! You're done working (or at least able to work less). It's time to bring your retirement vision to life—the one you've thoughtfully shaped over the past several years. Your preplanning activities helped you clarify your lifestyle goals, shed light on the financial realities, and laid the foundation. Your focused planning work during the final stretch helped you fine-tune the details.

Now comes the moment of truth—stepping into your Third Act and seeing how your plan truly fits your life.

In this chapter, we'll walk through the key transitions as you enter retirement and look at how your choices may evolve from here. Every piece of the puzzle we've explored so far comes into play. This is when you'll put your income strategy to the test, track your real expenses, and discover whether your budget holds up. It's also the perfect time to reflect on your purpose and values, especially if you're navigating this new chapter with a partner. And because your health is the foundation for everything else, we'll begin there.

Sign Up for Medicare and Focus on Your Health

A couple of months before you turn sixty-five, it's time to sign up for Medicare. Set your Medicare payments to auto-pay, so you never risk a lapse in coverage. Then double-check to be sure payments are going through; sometimes it takes a couple of tries to get everything synced in the not-so-smooth federal system.

Next, schedule the preventive care you need, including a physical, cancer screenings, and vision checks. Don't skip diagnostic appointments either. Catching an issue early, such as osteoporosis or early signs of Alzheimer's disease, can lead to early treatment and a better long-term outcome.

Start using your chosen Medicare plan and evaluate how well it works for you. Are your doctors attentive and thoughtful, or do you feel rushed and brushed off? Pay attention to your comfort and confidence in their care.

Also, consider healthcare logistics. How far are you from a hospital or urgent care facility? Even if you're in good health now, having nearby options can give you peace of mind. If something's not working, remember, you can make changes during Medicare's Open Enrollment Period each fall.

Is travel a big part of your retirement plan? Learn how your Medicare plan works when you travel to different states. If you're traveling internationally, you'll probably want to purchase a separate international healthcare policy to cover you when visiting other countries.

Most importantly, know that healthcare costs only go up. According to the health spending costs on the Peterson-KFF Health System Tracker, you should budget for at least a 4 percent annual increase. Each year is different, though. During the 2020 pandemic year average costs rose over 10 percent. If those statistics are a shock, remember, you can help keep those costs down by taking good care of yourself.

Time for New Health Habits

Are you already a healthy eater who stays active? If so, give yourself some credit—you've built a strong foundation for a vibrant retirement. If you're relocating, be intentional. Seek out local farmers' markets, regularly shop at grocery stores with fresh options, and find a nearby gym, pool, bike path, or walking trail to keep up the momentum.

If your health habits haven't been ideal, retirement is your golden opportunity to turn this around. Maybe a busy career led to too much fast food and too many skipped workouts. Now, that excuse is off the table—you finally have time to prioritize your well-being. Use it. You don't need to eat the way you did in your teenage years or during high school sports. Smaller portions, better nutrition, and mindful choices can go a long way for your health and for your budget.

If managing your weight feels like a challenge, talk with your doctor about options. Whether it's a support group, a referral to a dietitian, or trying a behavior-change app like Noom, help is out there.

Always wanted to try something new? This is your chance. Maybe you've moved near water and want to try paddleboarding, or you're in the mountains and hiking calls to you. Whether it's finding a walking group or joining an online fitness program, create a new routine that energizes you. And make it stick. Healthy habits aren't just good for your body—they're the key to enjoying this chapter to the fullest.

If budget is an issue, consider these tips:

- Take advantage of the many free online exercise videos for strength-training workouts, cardio, yoga, mat Pilates, and more.

- Invest in a sturdy pair of walking shoes and cruise your neighborhood, local parks, and walking paths in your area.

- Join free or low-cost classes through your local parks and recreation department, swimming pool, or senior center.

Retirement is your opportunity to develop or improve your health habits. Eating healthily, exercising, and being active is a ladder that leads to a fulfilling life in your golden years.

Retirement Depression: Signs and Remedies

Unfortunately, many retirees may struggle emotionally. In our research, we found studies noting that about one in four retirees report feeling depressed. For some, it's a continuation of preexisting mental health challenges. But for others, retirement brings a new kind of heaviness due to a loss of purpose, fear of the unknown, or feeling overwhelmed by the transition itself.

One of the best ways to avoid this emotional dip is to start with a solid plan. A well-thought-out plan provides structure, direction, and a sense of control. When you know what's ahead—even in broad strokes—you reduce anxiety and boost confidence. During your preplanning and planning stages, you've scouted out your future hometown, envisioned your dream lifestyle, and considered what day-to-day life will feel like beyond the initial retirement glow.

Still, unexpected challenges may arise. Maybe you're feeling lonely or disappointed that your new life isn't unfolding as you imagined. If so, it's time to act. Join local clubs, sign up for classes, or start volunteering in an area you care about.

BIG TIP: Purpose often lives where your interest meets contribution.

You can also find community online. Local Facebook groups, Meetup gatherings, and hobby-based forums are great places to find people who share your passions. If you're still struggling, don't go it alone. Therapy, support groups, mental health apps, such as Headspace, and honest conversations with friends and loved ones can make a huge difference.

One more thing: Financial stress can also fuel depression. If your budget is tighter than expected, take the time to reevaluate your expenses and look into resources that can help. Purpose, planning, connection, and financial peace of mind are potent antidotes to the retirement blues.

Maximizing Your Income

Hopefully, your retirement income isn't a surprise to you. You ran your income numbers a few years back and learned about the deductions from Social Security for Medicare and taxes. You know what's in your retirement accounts and what you'll need to take out in required minimum distributions.

Still, it's a huge transition. You go from earning paychecks to living off various types of savings and Social Security. It can feel scary, especially if you're among the majority of Americans who have saved $200,000 or less for retirement by age sixty-five. We found this frightening statistic in an Investopedia article titled "Here's How Much Americans Save for Retirement: How Do You Compare?" More frightening still, barely half of US households have a retirement account of any kind, according to a 2022 survey of consumer finances published by the Federal Reserve System.

As we discussed, if you possibly can, wait until your full vesting age to take Social Security. The difference in waiting for the higher benefit can add up to a small fortune over time, especially if you come from a long-lived family and might spend twenty or thirty years in retirement.

Whether you have minimal savings or different types of retirement accounts with substantial holdings, we strongly encourage you to talk with your financial advisor at this point. If you have multiple retirement accounts, you'll want to create an overarching strategy for your investments and financial plan, including taking required withdrawals, to help you reduce taxes and maximize spending money.

If you're a pension fund holder, you may have options on how to take your money—as a lump sum, for a limited time span, or monthly over your lifetime. This is another good conversation to have with a finance pro.

During your retirement, you may be tempted to withdraw more than the minimum required from your IRA to cover a large expense, such as a home remodel or lengthy European vacation. An advisor can help you understand if you have the wiggle room or whether that withdrawal would put your retirement plan in jeopardy.

There's one other way to get more cash from your retirement savings. That's by changing how it's invested.

Investing While Retired

People have different ideas about retirement investing. Some retirees want to be more conservative; since their earning years are over, they don't want to take any risk. Americans are living longer, so some retirees are staying aggressively invested to help fund their retirement into their nineties and beyond. Still others who've invested in rental property simply keep that rolling and collect their rents.

What you do may depend on many factors, including:

- How much money you have when you retire
- Your investing experience
- How long you expect to live
- Your interest in spending time on investing activities, either independently or with an investment advisor

The stories below, from a group of our relatives, show how varied the investing approaches can be in your retirement years.

———————— ☕ ————————

Nancy recently hit retirement age. She is a former financial reporter who knows a lot about how stock markets operate. She learned an income-focused investing system from an expert she interviewed and now uses his system to manage her money. The catch? This system requires active trading. She's usually online every weekday, trading in and out of securities. For Nancy, it's an interesting hobby. She devotes a few hours a week to this engaging activity, and she doesn't have to pay manager fees.

Her favorite thing about this approach is that, thanks to the high yields she earns, she never has to worry about whether the stock market is trending up or down. She collects her dividends either way. Those dividends represent spendable cash, not "paper profits" from market-value growth.

Nancy's ninety-three-year-old father, Morris, has been invested in a single Vanguard mutual fund since he retired at sixty-five. It has done well for decades, so he feels no need to diversify, even though this would be standard financial advice. At this point in life, he doesn't have many expenses, and his account is delivering all he needs. So, why change?

Nancy told us the story of her maternal grandparents who owned rental properties in the Los Angeles area that funded their retirement. Rents kept going up, and this created a great cash flow for Dottie and Jack while the properties continued to appreciate in value. Yes, they needed to budget

a certain amount to maintain the properties, but the continuous flow of income enabled them to live well in retirement.
They truly enjoyed their golden years together, traveling and
hosting many big family events.

As you can see, you can approach money management
in many different ways in your retirement. This is a great
topic to discuss with your financial advisor, especially if
you're worried that you haven't saved enough.

If you've found some of the information in this section confusing because you don't understand some of the
investing ideas, you have another task—learn more about
investing.

Invest Time to Learn About Your Investments

Retirement may be the first time in your life you're truly
in charge of your finances. Perhaps a company pension
handled the details, or your company's 401(k) offered just
a few options with limited decisions to make. Now, the
responsibility is yours, and that can feel both exciting and
a little daunting.

But don't let uncertainty keep you stuck. You're living
in the best era ever to learn about money. Free online
resources, online courses, and local seminars make financial education more accessible than ever. Dive in. Take a
class or two. Meet regularly with your financial advisor
and ask a lot of questions. Start closing the gaps in your
knowledge, step by step.

Keep in mind that some financial seminars are designed
to sell services. Learn from a variety of sources before

committing to any investment strategy. Recall our story of the financial seminar we attended, featuring a substandard presentation that didn't feel trustworthy. Always trust your instincts, and don't rush into anything under pressure.

You can find a world of information from credible websites, such as Morningstar Investor, Investor's Business Daily, Money, and Seeking Alpha.

BIG TIP: Think of financial literacy as part of your personal growth in retirement. The more you learn, the more empowered and confident you'll feel. As you invest wisely, you give yourself the best chance to keep your money growing—because life gets more expensive, but your potential to thrive doesn't have to shrink.

Budget Tweaks to Stay on Track

Retirement expenses have a funny way of adding up to more than you imagined they would, like the rising health-care premiums we mentioned earlier.

If you're running in the red and you've exhausted your opportunities to add income, it's time to implement some cost-cutting strategies. Start with the low-hanging fruit—any debt you've brought with you into retirement.

How to Deal with Debt

Many people think they're stuck with their debts. Often, that's not true. It's worth resolving any debts you can because outstanding debt lowers your credit rating, which makes it more expensive for you to borrow. In addition, the burden of debt can cause stress and anxiety, spoiling an otherwise vibrant retirement.

If you have any outstanding debt, say, from credit cards or past hospital bills, you can negotiate with debt collectors. They would rather have a portion than nothing at all. Here's a story on this topic with a happy ending.

———————— ☕ ————————

When a friend's husband passed away a few years ago, she was left with over $8,000 in medical bills. Catherine didn't feel up to talking to her creditors. Tracy wanted to help, so she contacted the creditors on Catherine's behalf.

"This woman is ill herself," Tracy told them. "She has $5,000 she can pay, or it'll be nothing at all." (A trick she learned from another friend.)

The creditors took the payout. Removing that debt took a large burden off Catherine's shoulders in her retirement.

Are you carrying balances on multiple credit cards and feeling overwhelmed? Explore balance transfer offers that can help you roll your debt into one manageable monthly payment, often with lower interest. You can also call your credit card companies directly. Many are willing to work with you and may reduce your rate just because you asked.

If your debt feels unmanageable, consider credit counseling. Be cautious—this field has its share of bad actors. But reputable nonprofit agencies have established relationships with creditors and can often negotiate better terms on your behalf. They'll work with you to create a repayment plan that fits your budget and helps you get back on track. Be sure to choose a well-regarded credit counseling service.

Dial Down Your Expenses

Once you've resolved any debts you can, look at the rest of your budget. All the things you might have cut back on earlier in life will also enable you to reduce monthly expenses now. Here's a list of budget items to consider:

- **Mortgage or rent**—Live somewhere cheaper or take in a renter.

- **Eating out**—Cut back on frequency, look for deals, eat at cheaper places, and meet friends for lunch instead of dinner.

- **Groceries**—Use coupons, switch to a store that offers more discounts and sales, and buy in bulk.

- **Travel**—Take fewer or less expensive trips, sign up on bargain travel sites, and stick to a predetermined budget when traveling.

- **Entertainment**—Enjoy movies, plays, and other events on bargain days and during bargain times, such as previews, matinees, or midweek tickets. Take advantage of free concerts in the park and other free or cheap activities.

- **Clothing and accessories**—Price compare, shop online deal sites, and don't buy a new item on impulse, especially if you don't need it.

- **Streaming services and other monthly subscriptions**—Keep your favorites only.

- **Transportation**—Sell a car, walk or bike more, and take public transportation.

You get the idea. Write down every cent you spend for a month and then decide what you can live without.

Don't overspend in your early retirement years. Those depleted savings mean you have less money to invest and grow, and you've increased the odds you'll end up outliving your savings. Instead, learn to be happy with a lifestyle you can afford. You'll enjoy many more stress-free retirement years.

Wake Up to Joy

As we wrap up this book, we thought we'd add a few more notes about ourselves—your coauthors—and our retirement journey. We hope our experience offers some insights and, possibly, some inspiration for you.

During this Third Act, we're continually focused on building a meaningful retirement life as individuals and as a couple—one grounded in deep friendships, strong family ties, a clear sense of purpose, and passions that keep us engaged. Writing this book has been a natural extension of our journey.

Planning for retirement gave us clarity about money and about the life we truly want to live. (Admittedly, we should have started our retirement preplanning five years ago!) This clarity inspired us to help others do the same. We are already traveling and talking with people about how to make their retirement more fulfilling and secure.

Taking the time to intentionally shape this Third Act has helped us grow more confident and content. We have deepened the relationships that matter to us and have come to understand which connections no longer serve us—and that's OK. There's freedom in that awareness, too.

While researching and writing this book on retirement, Chris realized it was important to be completely transparent with his kids. He explained what he has saved and let them know what they can expect to inherit. That conversation lifted a weight off his shoulders—and theirs, too.

Individually, and then together as a couple, we took the time to manage our finances. This means we wake up each morning with peace of mind. We know where our money's going and what our budget looks like, and we are secure in knowing that we've saved enough to enjoy the freedom we worked hard for, especially when it comes to travel. Knowing we've built a secure future that reflects our values gives us a sense of calm we wish for everyone.

Retirement planning isn't just about money. It's about peace of mind, having a purpose, and living your values every day.

Top Ten Takeaways for Your Retirement Success

Here's our final top ten list for your move from worker bee to retiree:

1. **Medicare signup**—Evaluate your choices and know when to sign up to avoid penalties.

2. **Your health**—Commit to preventive care, healthy eating, and regular exercise.

3. **Compare notes**—If you're in a marriage or partnership, make sure your retirement goals align.

4. **Focus on values and purpose**—Choose activities that make you feel good.

5. **Stay in touch with your feelings**—Watch for any signs of depression and get help if needed.

6. **Maximize your income**—Learn to make smart withdrawals from your retirement account.

7. **Choose an investment philosophy**—Decide whether you'll stay the course, be more conservative in your approach, or keep growing your savings aggressively.

8. **Keep learning about investing**—It's an ever-changing field, and you need to keep your money growing.

9. **Finalize your retirement budget**—Reduce debt and cut costs that don't bring you joy.

10. **Plan ahead**—Advance planning is your ticket to a retirement you'll love.

Remember, the accompanying workbook on our website includes all these top takeaway lists and much more. Visit www.YourRetirementWakeUp.com to download this free, helpful workbook.

Step Into Your Vibrant Retirement

"Life is like riding a bicycle. To keep your balance, you must keep moving."
—ALBERT EINSTEIN

Congratulations! You've taken the time to learn life-changing strategies to ensure you enjoy a healthy, wealthy retirement with a clear sense of purpose. If you weren't thinking about retirement before reading this book, you're now awake to the fact that it's coming—and that it takes planning to create the retirement life you'll love.

Whatever "great retirement" means to you, we want you to have options, not be stuck with few choices due to a limited budget. If you take one new step toward the retirement of your dreams, we'll consider this book a success. Maybe you'll save more, invest smarter, take better care of yourself, or get more clarity on your purpose in life. Improving any of these key elements will help you create a more fulfilling retirement, and we'll be cheering you on.

Again, we are not here as professionals in any of the fields we've spoken about. But we have been through the retirement mill, and we hope you can learn at least one thing from our mistakes and hard-won lessons. We hope you can grab a nugget or two of knowledge that will make your retirement life more fulfilling and secure.

As we send you off to put your retirement plan into action, we'll leave you with a few parting thoughts:

- Watch out for the chutes and ladders of life. Look for opportunities that jump you ahead, and run what-if scenarios to plan for unforeseen setbacks.

- Start now—no matter how old you are, you must start saving for and planning your retirement. Start educating yourself through online resources, mentors, or certified professionals. Then take action. The sooner you begin, the better off you'll be. Don't fall victim to the *mañana* effect.

- Taxes, healthcare costs, home insurance, and other expenses differ by state. Be sure to understand costs

and state rules and regulations wherever you contemplate retiring.

- Learn how to budget and handle your day-to-day finances. Your detailed knowledge of your income and expenses will build confidence and help you build a better financial nest egg for retirement.

- Seek professional financial help for investing advice. Don't be intimidated about finding a financial professional to help you. Seek a credentialed pro you trust as you look for ways to invest and grow your money.

- Don't rely on Social Security as your primary source of retirement income. When (or if) it arrives, consider it a bonus. Keep an eye on Social Security changes as they may be significant in coming years.

- Watch for health insurance and Medicare changes. These programs keep evolving.

- Take care of your mental and physical health. It's important at every life stage, and it's never too late to take better care of yourself.

- Know your values and develop strong EQ skills. These will enable you to make better decisions about your future.

- Establish transparency about family finances. Discussions about money and end-of-life planning with your parents and adult children can be challenging, but they're essential conversations that need to happen.

- Think about the impact your retirement plan will have on your family, especially your adult children.

For example, if you're planning to move closer to your kids and grandkids, be sure to have a frank discussion about your plans. Your wish for close proximity and a daily presence in their lives may not align with their lifestyle or preference.

- Plan your retirement with *purpose* in mind. Find something fulfilling to occupy your time, something that makes you excited to jump out of bed in the morning. You worked hard for this time in your life. Make it matter.

Now that you've read this book and heard our wake-up call, you know just how important it is to plan ahead for retirement. The ball is in your court to take the steps that lead to a great Third Act. You have all the insights you need to make it happen. We wish you a wonderful, fulfilling retirement—one that is healthy, wealthy, and brimming with a clear sense of purpose and joy!

Acknowledgments

It's amazing how retirement caught us by surprise. We grappled with nuts-and-bolts aspects, such as navigating Medicare to choose the right plan. And we started discussing the less tangible aspects of retirement, such as ensuring we both have a clear sense of purpose in our retirement years. What is the compelling activity, hobby, or work or volunteer job that will make us want to jump out of bed first thing in the morning?

We realized we weren't ready for retirement. As we began to talk with others, we found that we weren't alone. The number of people unprepared for the realities of retirement is staggering. That realization is what brought us to create this book. Thank you to all the friends, family, colleagues, and even strangers who were willing to serve as our sounding boards and share their personal experiences. You let us play the role of amateur social scientists, testing ideas and exploring strategies. Your stories and feedback are embedded in every page.

Special thanks to John Boccuzzi Jr. for your generous guidance and steady encouragement and for sharing your hard-won wisdom from your publishing journey. Your insights and reassurance when we needed it most made this process smoother and far more meaningful. We're deeply grateful for your support and friendship through the decades.

We also want to express deep appreciation to our long-time friend, Art Athans. Your encouragement planted the earliest seed for this book. Our thoughtful conversations led to your suggestion that we turn our retirement insights into something lasting—a legacy. We're grateful for the spark. You are the definition of living with purpose in retirement.

We also want to express our gratitude to Sara Stanich, founder of Cultivating Wealth in New York. Your thoughtful guidance and expertise helped clarify many of our questions. We knew you were the person to call, and you didn't disappoint.

Thank you to our writing coach, Carol Tice, for organizing the structure of this book and assisting with technical research. Her support in navigating the complexities of the writing process helped clarify our vision and direction.

Finally, heartfelt thanks to the incredible team behind this book. Your talents, dedication, and belief in the message made it possible. This book would not exist without you.

Additional Resources
for Readers

We hope you've gained some insights for your retirement planning in this book. Here are the next steps to take on your retirement journey.

I. Visit Our Website for These Free Resources

- **A free workbook that accompanies this book**—We've gathered many of the action items and key questions to ask to plan your retirement into this comprehensive workbook.

- **"How to Have the Tough Talk: A Parent's Guide to Discussing Retirement, Money & Your Estate with Your Children"**—Holding an open conversation with your adult children about your retirement plans and finances is difficult but vital. This free guide will help.

- **"Raising Money-Smart Kids: A Parent's Guide to Building Wealth, Wisdom & Legacy from Ages 1 to 18"**—Money shouldn't be a taboo subject with kids. Download this guide and help them be money smart for life.

2. Hire Chris Ragot to Speak to Your Group

Chris brings an engaging energy to an essential topic—navigating the road to a fulfilling, secure retirement. He speaks to groups nationally, including at corporate events, where he shares strategies and inspires employees to plan and save for retirement.

Backed by decades of speaking experience, he shares stories and provides guidance for audience members to plan their vibrant, rewarding, and financially secure future. Whether at corporate events, conferences, or intimate gatherings, his message is clear—start planning now to take control of your tomorrow.

Drawing from personal experience and a career built on trust, innovation, and leadership, Chris shares invaluable insights and specific actions to help audience members plan for a future beyond their expectations—a retirement that is healthy, wealthy, and brimming with a clear sense of purpose and joy!

Scan this QR code to book an appointment with Chris—and to discuss bulk purchasing orders for *Your Retirement Wake-Up Call.*

"As a CEO, I've spent years planning for growth and managing risk. This book made me realize my retirement plan deserves the same intentional strategy. It's an innovative, refreshing take on retirement that everyone should read."

—ROB TROXEL, CHAIRMAN, PREMIER TRUCK RENTAL

About the Authors

CHRIS RAGOT has spent the past forty-five years in a wide range of business leadership roles. He currently serves as chairman and board director for several privately held companies. Over the years, he has held key executive positions in industrial manufacturing and distribution, including more than two decades as a CEO.

While his professional journey has provided him with valuable experience, Chris's passion now lies in helping others. With this book, he hopes to help Americans better navigate the path toward a fulfilling and secure retirement.

As a CEO and visionary thinker, Chris has earned a reputation for seeing potential in people before they see it in themselves—giving them the inspiration and confidence to achieve more. Now, alongside his partner and coauthor, Tracy Sullivan, Chris continues his mission to uplift and empower others, fostering meaningful conversations about financial security, personal growth, and the power of early retirement planning. He speaks nationally to audiences of all ages, sharing action steps to prepare for retirement. Companies often hire Chris to speak at their corporate events, sharing strategies and inspiring employees to save and plan for retirement.

TRACY SULLIVAN, a professionally trained photographer born and raised in Chicago, Illinois, brings a fresh perspective to retirement. With a passion for health, fitness, and wholistic well-being, she blends a woman's insights with a lighthearted approach to life's next chapter. She is passionate about helping people plan and enjoy a healthy, wealthy retirement—and enjoy a clear sense of purpose, so they wake up to joy every day in their golden years.

When she's not behind the camera, Tracy enjoys exploring the world with her partner and coauthor, Chris Ragot, and their beloved goldendoodle, WALL-E. Whether skiing, hiking, biking, or traveling, she finds joy in connecting with nature and nurturing the mind, body, and soul. Tracy and Chris believe values and purpose aren't just words on a page; they're a way of life.

Get more tools and insights for your retirement journey at www.YourRetirementWakeUp.com.